THE DYNAMICS

OF

CULTURE CHANGE

AN INQUIRY
INTO RACE RELATIONS
IN AFRICA

BY

BRONISLAW MALINOWSKI

EDITED BY PHYLLIS M. KABERRY

NEW HAVEN

YALE UNIVERSITY PRESS

LONDON · HUMPHREY MILFORD · OXFORD UNIVERSITY PRESS

1945

INTRODUCTION

THERE is little need for me to recapitulate here the achievements of Malinowski in the field of anthropology, the contributions which he made to it in knowledge, in methods of research, and in theory. His longest and most intensive period of field work was done in the Trobriand Islands during World War I and, although he wrote many detailed monographs on specific aspects of Trobriand culture, it was typical of the breadth of his scientific approach that he proceeded to develop the wider theoretical implications of his research in kinship, magic, religion, education, economics, and law. Moreover, in the process he formulated what has been called his functional theory of culture, and he constantly refined the techniques for its study. His seminars at the London School of Economics were unique, not only because they were attended by administrative officials, missionaries, and specialists in anthropology and allied subjects, but also because he had his own particular methods of instruction. For the exposition of his theories he devised and used a series of charts or tables which permitted of a synoptic analysis of all aspects of culture. They contained certain guiding principles and a condensed set of instructions for the fieldworker; and they compelled him to make as exhaustive a survey as possible of the community which he was sent out to study. They also constituted a scheme for the presentation and examination of data, a means by which his own theories and those of others could be tested, gaps in information revealed, and new avenues for research suggested.[1]

As an anthropologist who was truly international in his thinking Malinowski realized the importance of anthropology not only for the study of "primitive" peoples but also for an understanding of European and Oriental societies; and in his later years he devoted more and more of his energies to writing on war, nationalism, international coöperation, freedom, and democracy.[2] He addressed meetings on those subjects, and

1. For an example of his charts, the reader is referred to Malinowski's article, "The Scientific Basis of Applied Anthropology," Reale Accademia d'Italia, Fondazione Alessandro Volta, Estratto dagli Atti dell' VIII Convegno (Rome, 1938; published, 1940), pp. 18–19.

2. *Vide* Malinowski's articles, "The Deadly Issue," *Atlantic Monthly*, XLIII (December, 1936); "An Anthropological Analysis of War," *American Journal Sociology*, Vol. XLVI (1941); and also his book, *Freedom and Civilization* (New York, 1944).

he participated in those groups which were, and still are, attempting to formulate plans for postwar reconstruction and for some type of international federation and control. To these matters he brought not only the comparative knowledge and objectivity of a scientist but also his own humanism and European background.

As a person, keenly alive to the most urgent problems in his own particular field, Malinowski early drew attention to the need for a practical anthropology.[3] Later, in 1935, in his *Coral Gardens and Their Magic*, he made a specific reference to the influence of European culture on Trobriand beliefs and customs and stated: "The functional method, or at least that branch of it with which I am associated, was very largely born in the field. There I began to realize that even the reconstruction of all pre-European natives of some fifty or a hundred years ago is not the real subject-matter of field-work. The subject-matter of field-work is the changing Melanesian or African. He has already become a citizen of the world, is affected by contacts with the world-wide civilization, and his reality consists in the fact that he lives under the sway of more than one culture. The principle of studying the changing native as he really is enables us, on the one hand, to reconstruct his pre-European culture, not by guess-work or by fortuitously brushing away a piece of calico, a Christian belief, an irksome European taboo, but by studying how these things work, how they clash with his original culture, or else how they have been incorporated into it. On the other hand, the process of diffusion of culture, as it is going on under our very eyes, is one of the most important historical events in the development of mankind. To neglect its study is definitely to fail in one of the most important tasks of Anthropology." [4]

In 1934, Malinowski gave an address in Capetown on "Native Education and Culture Contact," [5] and he then made an extensive trip through East and South Africa carrying out an anthropological survey for five months among the Babemba, Swazi, Chaga, Masai, Kikuyu, and Maragoli tribes. He continued to publish articles on culture change, to lecture in England, Europe, and the United States; to discuss and work out methods for its study in his seminars both at the London School at Economics and at Yale University. Finally, he was for many years associated with the International Institute of African Languages

---

3. *Vide* Malinowski, "Practical Anthropology," *Africa*, Vol. II (1929). For Malinowski's other articles on culture contact and change, the reader is referred to the bibliography at the end of this book.

4. Malinowski, *Coral Gardens and Their Magic* (1935), I, 480–481.

5. The substance of this address was published in the *International Review of Missions* (October, 1936).

and Cultures, an organization which has done much to further research
in colonial problems and culture change in Africa.

He early recognized that new methods were necessary for the study
of those communities undergoing intensive change and he elaborated
what, for the sake of brevity, may be termed his "three-column approach." By this means he projected data onto a table of three columns,
and thus brought out clearly the three phases of culture contact and
change: the impinging culture with its institutions, intentions, and interests; the reservoir of indigenous custom, belief, and living traditions;
and the processes of contact and change, where members of the two
cultures coöperate, conflict, or compromise. Basic to the understanding
of his approach to culture contact is his theory of the institution as
the "isolate" of culture, as the smallest cultural unit—"a group of people united for the pursuit of a simple or complex activity; always in
possession of a material endowment and a technical outfit; organized
on a definite legal and customary charter, linguistically formulated in
myth, legend, rule, and maxim; and trained or prepared for the carrying out of its task." [6] Hence contact becomes primarily the impact between institutions, in the process of which they are modified, assume
new forms or new functions.

Malinowski rarely used the word "acculturation," and in one of his
more recent writings he advocated the adoption of a term coined by
Don Fernando Ortiz, namely, "transculturation," since in this there
were "no implications of one standard dominating all the phases (of
culture change), but a transition in which both sides are active, each
contributing its quota, each merging into a new reality of civilization." [7] The phrase generally used by him was "culture contact and
change," and the definition which I have selected has been taken from
a typescript entitled *The Forces and Factors of Culture Change*, written for a lecture in Copenhagen in 1938. It appeared in the published
abstract as follows:

"Culture change is the process by which the existing order of society—its organization, beliefs and knowledge, tools and consumers'
goods—is more or less rapidly transformed. Change may be induced
either by factors and forces of spontaneous initiative and growth, or
by the contact of two different cultures. The result in the first instance

6. *Infra*, p. 50.
7. Malinowski, "Introduccion" to *Contrapunteo Cubano del Tabaco y el Azucar*, by
Fernando Ortiz (Havana, 1940), pp. xvi–xvii. Malinowski also employed this term in
his article, "The Pan-African Problem of Culture Contact," *American Journal of
Sociology*, XLVIII, No. 6 (1943), 650.

is a process of independent evolution; in the second, that which is usually called diffusion." [8]

It will be obvious to anyone familiar with his works and to readers of this book that diffusion had for him a connotation different from that attributed to it by many American, British, and German anthropologists. The significance attached to the term by him here derived necessarily from his own theory of culture, and implied a rejection of that concept which regards culture as a pattern of traits or trait-complexes. For him, the units of transformation are institutions, and in the process of change these assume new functions or new forms in response to the new needs engendered in the situation of contact. Hence, diffusion is a process of "reorganization on entirely new and specific lines." It is not "a mixture of cultural elements" which can be disentangled from their cultural matrix and traced back to their provenance in parent cultures.

For many years Malinowski had contemplated writing a book on culture contact and change, and since I had received a fellowship from Yale University to carry out research in Race Relations during the academic year 1942–43, he did me the honor of suggesting that I collaborate with him. His unexpected death shortly afterward made the realization of that project impossible, but Mrs. Malinowska handed over his manuscripts on culture change to me to edit, and, with the consent of Professor Maurice Davie, Chairman of the Department of Sociology at Yale, I undertook the task of arranging the papers for publication. Unfortunately, Malinowski had left no plans for the book,

---

8. *Vide* Malinowski, "The Dynamics of Contemporary Diffusion," a résumé published in *International Congress of Anthropological and Ethnological Sciences* (Copenhagen, 1939).

About the same time, Professors Redfield, Linton, and Herskovits formulated a definition of acculturation and culture change, which I include here for purposes of comparison:

"Acculturation comprehends those phenomena which result when groups of individuals having different cultures come into continuous first-hand contact, with subsequent changes in the original cultural patterns of either or both groups. . . .

"Under this definition, acculturation is to be distinguished from *Culture-change*, of which it is but one aspect, and *assimilation*, which is at times a phase of acculturation. It is also to be differentiated from *diffusion*, which, while occurring in all instances of acculturation, is not only a phenomenon which frequently takes place without the occurrence of the types of contact between peoples specified in the definition above, but also constitutes only one aspect of the process of acculturation. . . . Diffusion can be thought of as that aspect of cultural change which includes the transmission of techniques, attitudes, concepts, and points of view from one people to another; whether it be through the medium of a single individual or of a group, or whether the contact is brief or sustained" (*vide* M. J. Herskovits, *Acculturation: A Study of Culture Contact* [New York, J. J. Augustin, 1938], pp. 10, 14).

nor had we discussed them since we had decided to do nothing until the following October. As a former student of his I was, however, familiar with his theories and had attended his seminars on culture change at the London School of Economics during the period 1936–38.

Among his manuscripts there were fifteen folders containing a miscellaneous collection of notes dealing with culture contact and change, and written mostly between 1936 and 1938. These included typescripts of articles published in *Africa* and by the Reale Accademia D'Italia, together with alternative versions and additional material which had not been printed. There were abstracts and notes of lectures given at Oxford, Copenhagen, and Rome; typescripts of anything from two to twenty pages containing marginal notes and dealing with specific aspects such as witchcraft, nutrition, war, and so on; résumés of seminar discussions, synopses, preliminary drafts, charts, and penciled notes.

Since some of the material had already been published, two possibilities presented themselves for the arrangement of the text: either to collate the unpublished material as a long essay and include it in a monograph containing all his published articles on culture change; or to utilize as much as possible of all the material available and edit it as a complete book. Since there was much that was new, including a detailed exposition of the methods to be employed in field work, I chose the second alternative. The scope and framework of the book was based on some of his articles and his handling of the subject in the seminars which he held at Yale University in 1941. Part I incorporates much of the material in his "Introductory Essay" to *Methods of Study of Culture Contact in Africa* (1938),[9] which recorded some of the results of the research program carried out by the International Institute of African Languages and Cultures from 1931 on. Part II represents the application of his theory of culture contact and change to specific institutions.

For some chapters I had at my disposal fairly complete manuscripts which required only minor corrections and the insertion of additional notes or sections. This applied in particular to the second part of Chapter I, to Chapters II and the first part of III, to IV, VII, VIII, X, and XIII. Among the remainder, with the exception of XI and XII, I was dealing principally with typescript; but there was much rearrangement to be done, and they can be said to represent a mosaic of all materials available bearing on the subjects concerned. Chapters XI

9. *Africa;* and Memorandum XV, The International Institute of African Languages and Cultures (1938).

I should like to take the opportunity here to thank the International Institute of African Languages and Cultures for permission to reproduce the greater part of this article.

and XII, two of the most important in the book from the point of view of colonial administration, were the most difficult since, in the first case, notes were fairly full but in pencil; while in the second, there were only about eight pages all told, and some of these repetitious. Fortunately, however, there were detailed charts containing a synopsis of the facts, and these, with a little expansion, I incorporated into the text. For my own additions I have put a remark to that effect in footnotes. Apart from minor alterations which do not change the substance of his ideas, generalizations, criticisms, and theories, the wording of practically the whole book is that of Malinowski.

The reader of this book will see that Malinowski for the illustration of his theories and methods has drawn mainly on material from South Africa and the dependencies in East Africa which come under the direction of the Colonial Office of the United Kingdom. Had he lived he would, without doubt, have covered a wider field and also driven home the relevance of many of his generalizations on African culture contact for other parts of the world where communities are in process of change. He himself, in an introduction which he wrote in 1940 to Dr. Laura Thompson's *Fijian Frontier*, stated that a comparison of a number of monographs on culture change in different areas would reveal an astonishing similarity of processes and results.[10]

There is also one other point which should be stressed here. Malinowski, from 1929 onward, worked and fought for the recognition of "practical anthropology," and much of the credit must be given to him, along with those anthropologists whom he taught and influenced, for an increasing tendency in administrative and missionary circles to utilize anthropological advice and to require from their officials some training in anthropology. Even prior to the war, cadets of the administrative services of Papua and the Territory of New Guinea took a course in anthropology at the University of Sydney, and for many years a government anthropologist has been attached to the administrative staff in both dependencies. Recently, two anthropologists have been appointed to assist in native rehabilitation in those areas already freed from Japanese occupation, and they are concentrating, in particular, on problems of education and labor. In the United States, the new Indian policy launched by Commissioner John Collier of the Indian Office of Affairs has drawn heavily on anthropological knowledge. In England, in 1940, the Colonial Development and Welfare Act was passed, and under it £5 million a year for ten years has been set aside for the development and welfare of the dependencies of the United Kingdom. There is also an additional £500,000 a year allocated

10. Laura Thompson, *Fijian Frontier* (1940), pp. xxi–xxii.

for research. A Colonial Research Committee, under the chairmanship of Lord Hailey, has been appointed to organize research, to deal with applications and to initiate new schemes. In the Progress Report issued for 1942–43 the importance of practical anthropology is explicitly recognized:

Knowledge of the social and economic conditions and of the cultural characteristics of colonial peoples is necessary in the framing of all schemes of development, whether medical, agricultural, veterinary or educational, and for the planning of the general economic policy of a territory. Such data are very inadequate in the case of most colonial territories. The reasons are not hard to find. In this country the results of scientific investigations of social problems are only now being applied to the conduct of domestic policy. In the Colonies there have been special difficulties in carrying out such investigations. While all departments have naturally been concerned with social questions, none has been specially responsible for the conduct of detailed investigations in these fields, nor have departments of social studies yet been attached to colonial institutes of higher education. The recent provision of funds under the Act of 1940 for the setting up of a West African Institute to be attached to Achimota College will be a first experiment in the establishment of a regional centre of social and linguistic studies. . . . The Committee has encountered its own difficulties in dealing with this subject. . . . It has, therefore, been thought advisable to seek the advice of a number of groups of experts in particular spheres. They cover the following subjects: linguistics; demography, anthropology, social surveys; economics; systems of colonial laws; colonial administration; education and psychology. On the basis of the reports of these groups the organization of research in the social sciences will be further considered by the Committee.[11]

The launching of such schemes for research is clearly in line with the approach to native problems advocated by Malinowski in this book, and he would have been the first to welcome and acknowledge this new orientation in administrative policy. To the individuals involved in such projects there is little need to make a plea for an applied anthropology. Nevertheless, I have included Malinowski's arguments in this book, for there are still some anthropologists who would challenge the thesis that a practical anthropology can be scientific; while, on the other hand, among nonspecialists there is still too little realization of what anthropology can contribute; or else there is a refusal to face the issues brought to their notice by anthropologists. Among the specialists, Professor Herskovits, who has himself made a study of

11. Colonial Research Committee, *Progress Report,* 1942–43, cmd. 6486 (1943), p. 17.

acculturation, would question the scientific validity of research carried out by a European in those situations in which Europeans and Natives are in contact. Since this attitude constitutes something of a challenge to the premises of this book, I shall quote him in detail:

Are not anthropologists themselves, in devoting themselves to the study of the contact between their own culture and native civilizations, likewise in danger of narrowing, then, the point of view they have obtained? The uncritical tendency to see native cultures everywhere forced out of existence by the overwhelming drive of European techniques; the feeling that these "simpler folk" must inevitably accept the sanctions of their more efficient rulers as they do some of the outward modes of life of those under whose control they live; all these reflect a type of ethocentrism that should be absent from the scientific studies of an anthropologist. It is for this reason, that to realize to the utmost the scientific gain to be had from studies of culture contact, those situations where nations of Europe or America were or are today in no way involved should be first sought out for study, since here the student who comes from these countries can in no wise identify himself with the process he is studying. In this manner scientific objectivity will be enhanced; otherwise in its study of cultures in contact, anthropology must suffer, without check, from the same handicaps under which other social sciences labour in neglecting to look beyond the horizon of our culture.

And again:

It is apparent from the analyses of work in the field of culture contact that a first requirement is for studies to be made among peoples where the student can least identify himself with the issues at stake. In terms of acculturation research, this means that the prime necessity is for investigation to be carried out among folk whose contacts involve no European or American group. A number of likely localities are available where the cultures cannot only be studied under conditions of contact, but in related forms prior to contact.[12]

With the first part of Herskovits' statement, his criticism of the ethnocentric anthropologist, I am in complete agreement. Undoubtedly, anthropological books have been written in which the writers have indulged in pro-Native ranting and expressed the fear that Native peoples are bound to succumb in the struggle with the forces of European civilization. But such books now represent a minority, and scarcely justify his pessimistic, if not derogatory, view of the degree of detachment that can be attained and maintained by the anthropologist. Within recent years both British and American anthropolo-

12. Herskovits, *op. cit.*, pp. 31–32, 120.

gists have published work which proves that the objectivity acquired in scientific training and in the field can be carried over into situations where an analysis of our cultural institutions is also demanded. Many of these contain a detached examination of European policy, and a realistic assessment of the issues and difficulties inherent in change. A discussion of the value of some of these contributions, together with a formulation of the methods and principles of an applied anthropology, will be found in the chapters of this book.[13]

Herskovits' suggestion that studies be carried out only where European or American culture does not enter into the situation lacks realism, since there are few communities left which have not felt the impact, in one form or another, of Western civilization. Were his advice followed in this matter, apparently the processes of change occurring in the greater part of the world at present would be consigned to future generations of anthropologists as a problem in historical reconstruction!

Malinowski was keenly aware of the difficulties in studying culture contact in Africa and of maintaining an attitude of scientific detachment. But just because change is so widespread and rapid, and represents the dominant characteristic of most African societies, the problem was a challenge to him as a scientist, and he responded as a scientist: first, by emphasizing the need for an objective study of existing conditions; and secondly, by working out new methods for the analysis of the complexities of culture change in all its aspects. His theory of culture and his examination of the forces which come into play when two cultures impinge upon each other will be found in this book. His approach is essentially dynamic in that he views the contact situation in terms of stresses and strains, of conflict and coöperation, and of compromise and passive resistance; or, to phrase it differently, in terms of the persistence of old institutions, the process of modification in others, and the gradual evolution of new ones in which members of both cultures participate. To handle this data he elaborated the synoptic tables to which I have earlier referred. While this type of study and these techniques can be refined further and supplemented by the use of psychological tests, by the study of the psychological mechanisms of selection and integration in culture change,[14] and by

13. Outside the books mentioned by Malinowski for the African area, there are also a number of first-rate monographs and articles which have been written on culture contact where Europeans are involved. Among these one might cite the work of Keesing, Buck, Hogbin, Firth, Mead, Groves, Elkin, F. E. Williams, Beaglehole, Reed, Powdermaker, Dollard, and many others.

14. Herskovits, "Memorandum for the Study of Acculturation," *American Anthropologist*, XXXVIII, n.s. (1936), 152.

an analysis of why some cultures are more resistant to contact than others,[15] it is obvious that we have in Malinowski's method one which is applicable not only to contemporary change in Africa but to other areas of the world: to contact between Native tribes, or between European nations; or to problems involved in the assimilation of immigrant groups; or to the gradual urbanization of rural districts.

Acknowledgments

I wish to express my warmest thanks to Yale University not only for a Research Fellowship in Race Relations which enabled me to edit Malinowski's manuscripts on culture change but also for the facilities and assistance which were extended to me so freely during my stay in New Haven. The work was carried out in consultation with Professor Maurice R. Davie, Chairman of the Departments of Sociology and of Race Relations at Yale, and I am only too keenly conscious of the many demands which I made on his time, kindness, and patience. I owe much to him for his advice and helpful criticsm of this book.

I am also greatly indebted to Dr. Audrey Richards, Dr. Lucy Mair, Dr. Margaret Read, and Dr. Raymond Firth who, in spite of their extra duties and work connected with the war, read through the preliminary draft of the manuscript and offered comments and criticism. While I was unable to agree to all their suggestions, many proved of the utmost value in my later revision of the book.

Finally, I should like to express my deep gratitude to Mrs. A. V. Malinowska for entrusting me with the privilege and responsibility of editing her husband's manuscripts, and for the advice and encouragement which she has at all times given me. It is a task which I have undertaken gladly for, as an erstwhile student of Malinowski's, I realize how much he contributed to my knowledge and to my training in theory and field work. The debt which I owe to one who was a great anthropologist and a generous friend can never be repaid; but I hope in editing his manuscripts I have made available to other anthropologists and to future students the measure of his contribution to one of the most important fields of anthropology—that of culture contact and change.

                                                            P. M. K.

London, 1944.

15: Ruth Benedict, "Two Patterns of Indian Acculturation," *American Anthropologist*, XLV, n.s. (1943), 207 ff.

CONTENTS

CHARTS

TABLES

PART ONE

I

THE NEW TASKS OF MODERN ANTHROPOLOGY

The Need for an Applied Anthropology

Culture change is the process by which the existing order of a society, that is, its social, spiritual, and material civilization, is transformed from one type into another. Culture change thus covers the more or less rapid processes of modification in the political constitution of a society; in its domestic institutions and its modes of territorial settlement; in its beliefs and systems of knowledge; in its education and law; as well as in its material tools and their use, and the consumption of goods on which its social economy is based. In the widest sense of the term, culture change is a permanent factor of human civilization; it goes on everywhere and at all times. It may be induced by factors and forces spontaneously arising within the community, or it may take place through the contact of different cultures. In the first instance it takes the form of *independent evolution;* in the second it constitutes that process which in anthropology is usually called *diffusion.*

Just now, however, culture change has assumed in both its variants a rapidity and magnitude unprecedented in human history. The technical inventions, the developments of industrial enterprise and of financial and mercantile organization have speeded up evolution in the Western world, giving it a far-reaching mastery of the material environment. Mechanical progress, however, has not been paralleled by a corresponding control of social conditions and spiritual culture. The Western world is divided by war and by the danger of new wars; by an acute strife in political principle and by the inability in most countries to cope with some of the most urgent economic difficulties. The so-far insoluble problems of world economics and politics, of international law and nationalist reaction, are a phase of culture change. But the anthropologist has not been called upon to deal with these questions in the spirit of detached research and scientific insight which might perhaps be of value to future generations. He may be allowed for the moment to indicate that some conclusions, valid and valuable with reference to primitive peoples, might also be successfully applied to our own societies. The anthropologist could also usefully reflect on the fact that evolution and diffusion are processes not so different as they appear at first sight. Culture change in Africa does not differ profoundly from that which is at present transforming the rural and backward countries of Europe from peasant communities, living by indigenous age-long economic systems, by folklore and kinship organization, into a new type closely akin to the proletariat found in the industrial districts of the United States, England, or France.

But for many reasons it is simpler and more profitable to study the processes of diffusion in a field which, being more remote, can be worked upon with greater detachment, and where the questions are at the same time simpler and under the more direct control of the agents of change. It is also best to select a wide but well-defined area for our study, and one on which a body of research on culture change has already been in progress for the last few years. In Africa we have had of late a number of studies on the broad movement which is taking place as from tribal conditions toward the partial westernization of the Natives.[1]

The anthropologist is becoming increasingly aware that the study of culture change must become one of his main tasks in field work and theory. The figment of the "uncontaminated" Native has to be dropped from research in field and study. The cogent reason for this is that the "uncontaminated" Native does not exist anywhere. The

1. In this, the initiative came from the International Institute of African Languages and Cultures, which to a large extent also financed the work. It was carried out, among others, by Dr. A. I. Richards of Johannesburg University and Dr. M. Read of the London School of Economics; Dr. I. Schapera of the University of Capetown; Dr. M. Hunter, Dr. S. Nadel, and Dr. Gordon Brown; Dr. L. P. Mair of the London School of Economics; Mr. Godfrey Wilson, Director of the Rhodes-Livingstone Institute (N. Rhodesia); Dr. M. Fortes, Dr. G. Wagner, and Dr. K. Oberg—all of whom were trained in the Department of Anthropology, University of London.

From Johannesburg, under the guidance of Professor Winifred Hoernlé, the study of detribalized communities in the Union has been carried out by Mr. and Mrs. Krige, Mrs. Hellman, and Mrs. H. Beemer, who worked among the tribal and detribalized sections of the Swazi.

A special contribution to the theory and methods in the study of contact and change is Memorandum XV, of the International Institute of African Languages and Cultures, entitled *Methods of Study of Culture Contact in Africa* (London, 1938), reprinted from *Africa*, Vols. VII, VIII, IX.

All the recent volumes of *Africa*, the journal of the Institute, must, however, be consulted by anyone interested in modern problems of practical anthropology, especially those of culture change.

man of science has to study what is, and not what might have been. When his main interest lies in the reconstruction of the tribal past, he still has to study the Native as he is now, affected by Western influences. Only on the basis of what remains of the old culture, as well as by tapping the memories of old informants and by scanning old records, can he infer the preëxisting tribal conditions and proceed to the reconstruction of the past.

The modern student, however, is also aware that in order to appreciate what diffusion is it is necessary to study it empirically and at firsthand. Thus field work on the large-scale diffusion in present-day Africa becomes a scientific task in its own right. It is the duty of the ethnologist, as a chronicler of contemporary events, to describe and analyze one of the most significant phases in human history, that is, the present westernization of the world. Observations on culture change, as it happens under our eyes, reveal to us also the general laws of diffusion; they provide the materials for the understanding of certain aspects of human culture: the tenacity of beliefs and traditional modes of life; the reasons why certain aspects of culture diffuse more rapidly than others—in short the dynamic character of the process.

As a humanist, he ought to be aware that in this process there are involved human interests and passions that are still largely under the full control of agents of the active Western civilization. This control has not always been scientifically enlightened by a knowledge of all the facts at issue. Even now we must ask: are the changes in Native societies such as to bring about a common existence of harmonious coöperation; or must they lead to temporarily suppressed but powerful forces of coming disruption, upheaval, and historical catastrophe on an unprecedented scale?

There is a moral obligation to every calling, even to that of a scientific specialist. The duty of the anthropologist is to be a fair and true interpreter of the Native. This is not merely a duty of gratitude for favors received in the form of information, good-will and generosity —though even this would put the student of primitive mankind under a specific obligation. It is evidence of the fact that the fieldworker understands or should understand the conditions under which Native races live. He ought to be able to make clear to traders, missionaries, and exploiters what the Natives really need and where they suffer most under the pressure of European interference. There is no doubt that the destiny of indigenous races has been tragic in the process of contact with European invasion. We speak glibly about the "spread of Western civilization," about "giving the Natives the benefit of our own culture," about the "Dual Mandate," and the "White Man's Burden."

In reality, the historian of the future will have to register that Europeans in the past sometimes exterminated whole island peoples; that they expropriated most of the patrimony of savage races; that they introduced slavery in a specially cruel and pernicious form; and that even if they abolished it later, they treated the expatriated Negroes as outcasts and pariahs.

The Native still needs help. The anthropologist who is unable to perceive this, unable to register the tragic errors committed at times with the best intentions, at times under the stress of dire necessity, remains an antiquarian covered with academic dust and in a fool's paradise. Can research be of any practical use? It has often been the practice in some African colonies, wherever irremediable harm has been done, or affairs have reached an impasse, to summon a "commission of scientific inquiry," in reality to help save the face of the government and to deaden the pangs of conscience. But research in order to be of use must be inspired by courage and purpose. It must be briefed by that constructive statesmanship and wise foresight which establish the relevant issues and have the courage to apply the necessary remedies.

Shall we, therefore, mix politics with science? In one way, decidedly "yes," because if knowledge gives foresight and foresight means power, it is a universal stultification of scientific results to insist that they can never be useful or used by those who have influence. The importance of culture contact and change as a subject of research has been recognized in most countries where colonial affairs are of practical importance, and anthropology flourishes. Historically, perhaps, the palm of priority belongs to Holland, where it is sufficient to name such pioneers as C. Snouck Hurgronje, who was able both to preach and to practice the value of anthropology in the fair and rational treatment of Natives; C. van Vollenhoven, whose interest in customary law was as theoretically revealing as it has become practically influential; the ethnographic work of missionaries and administrators, as well as the more recent influence of such experienced administrators as van Eerde and Schrieke.

The prewar German Colonial Office encouraged ethnographic studies, although it did not have time to combine the results of scientific knowledge with improvements in administrative policy to any large extent. But in Germany such leading students of primitive cultures and languages as Westermann and Thurnwald discovered early in their scientific careers the importance, both theoretical and practical, of studies in culture change.

In France, the work of Delafosse, Labouret, and Maunier proves that culture change and contact problems are being considered by students and practical men alike.

Finally, in Great Britain and the United States, interest in culture change has of late become dominant. The names of W. H. R. Rivers and of Captain G. H. L. F. Pitt-Rivers head the list among early British scholars. The work of the Departments of Anthropology at Sydney and Capetown, under the initiative of A. R. Radcliffe-Brown; the teaching and research at Cambridge, London, and Oxford; the special interest shown in culture change and applied anthropology by the Royal Anthropological Institute—all have started almost simultaneously with the American initiative associated with the names of Wissler, Redfield, Parsons, Herskovits, and Radin; as well as P. H. Buck (Te Rangi Hiroa) and Felix Keesing working at Honolulu. The International Institute of African Languages and Cultures has, since its foundation in 1926, made an attempt to take the question beyond national boundaries and, avoiding all political issues, has organized research on problems of contact in all African colonies, with the coöperation of science, missionary enterprise, and the administrative agencies of all the countries concerned.[2]

Unfortunately, however, there is still a strong but erroneous opinion in some circles that practical anthropology is fundamentally different from theoretical or academic anthropology. The truth is that science begins with applications. A physicist or chemist or biologist knows this by heart. What is application in science and when does "theory" become practical? When it first allows us a definite grip on empirical reality; in other words, as soon as a theory is true, it is also "applied" in the sense that it is experimentally confirmed. Give and take between human mastery and intervention on the one hand, and the course of natural events on the other, is the only solid foundation for experimental science. It is enough to remember how the revolutionary, though at first strictly theoretical, discoveries of Galvani and Volta have through the subsequent contributions of Ampère and Faraday, of Kelvin and Marconi, transformed our control of electricity and of the ether. The stupendous achievements of modern engineering are the legitimate lineal outcome of the detached and disinterested inquiries into the nature of force, space, and time inaugurated by the Pole Copernicus, the Italians Galileo and Torricelli, the Frenchman Des-

2. In several parts of Africa, governments have enlisted the services of anthropologists for special surveys. Noteworthy in this respect has been the work of Dr. C. K. Meek and Mr. P. Talbot in Nigeria; of Mr. Gordon Brown and Mr. Bruce Hutt in Tanganyika; of Mrs. H. Beemer in Swaziland; and of Professor and Mrs. Seligman and Dr. Evans Pritchard in the Anglo-Egyptian Sudan. Ed.

cartes, the Englishman Newton, the Hollander Huygens, and the German Leibnitz. Exactly as in ordinary engineering no aspect of physical theory is irrelevant, so also social engineering is simply the empirical aspect of social theory.

Thus scientific anthropology must be practical. Here comes an immediate corollary: the scientific anthropologist must be the anthropologist of the changing Native. Why? Because what exists nowadays is not a primitive culture in isolation but one in contact and process of change. In so far as reconstruction is attempted at all it must be on the basis of what can be studied in the present. A discussion of trends or tendencies of change will be a theoretical and constructive by-product of observation. The very essence of history is that it has a future as well as a past. If anthropology has been very often an escape into the exotic, history has often remained the shelter for those who prefer their past dead and buried to tradition alive and active. The antiquarian and romantic tendency toward the retrospective and reconstructive is often nothing but an evasion of the real issues. In natural science the student looks for fundamental forces—mechanical, chemical, electromagnetic —very largely in order to harness them for man's future use. In sociology the criteria of relevance, power, and vitality are at least as important. Once we realize that, we see that the anthropologist faced with the study of culture change cannot ultimately evade the big practical problems which belong to constructive colonial statesmanship.[3]

The field of culture change is one in which it is impossible to keep apart the theoretical and practical issues involved. The practical man is interested in culture change, the administrator in political and legal adjustments, the missionary in the change of religion and morals, the settler and the entrepreneur in the possibilities of labor, indigenous production and consumption. The motives and interests of Europeans engaged in government, work, or disinterested teaching and evangelizing are, of course, not scientific, but they are obviously an intrinsic part of the present situation in Africa and elsewhere. Not only that; it is possible to show that most of the interests and motives of the practical agencies in Africa can be formulated into problems which are

---

3. The relevance of anthropology for administrative problems has also been stressed by Lord Hailey in *An African Survey* (1938), p. 43, where he states: "The study of African reactions to European culture, in such matters as marriage, inheritance, the private ownership of land, and the sanctions of law and order, is perhaps the most important aspect of anthropological work to-day." It is admitted, however, that "governments have, as a rule, given little direct support to specific inquiry of the type above described, either by the creation of a post of government anthropologist or by subsidizing the work of research students" (p. 45). Ed.

not at all different from those of the sociologist. The prospector who wants to make his pile and then run away need not worry how far his activity arouses ill feeling, the distrust of Europeans, race hatred, or even serious economic distress. The settler who thinks of the future and the generations to come will have to keep in mind problems of future race relations, will have to avoid serious injury or even insult to the Black neighbors of his own White children. The question of the health or even the survival of African tribes, of a sound community life emerging gradually out of the chaos of detribalization, the problem of how certain changes in Native law will give rise to serious maladjustments, how far sexual morality is to be debased with the best intentions —all this interests the sociologist and the practical man in the same measure.

In the study of culture change we have other reasons why the practical side is specially fruitful to research, and why the full coöperation of the European agencies in Africa is necessary for the intelligent study of all problems. The reason for this is that in colonial policies we have perhaps the nearest approach to an experiment, at times almost a controlled experiment, to be found in social science. In administration, for instance, the principle of Indirect Rule is one where definite practical results are anticipated on good theoretical grounds. To study academically what happens under the various experiments in Indirect Rule without being acquainted with the practical difficulties and the anticipations of smooth working would obviously mean shutting one's eyes to the really dynamic side of the whole question.

Thus Native administration has to plan clearly the system of law, which will be always a combination of Native custom and European principles of justice, and then apply this system. The financiers have also to organize taxation and to budget for expenditure in hygiene and in education. In all this, we have on the one hand planning and on the other a process by which the qualities as well as the imperfections, the difficulties and the success of the planning are being verified. The anthropologist who is not allowed to penetrate fully into the inner councils of administrative policies will lose a valuable opportunity of observing how a social experiment works.

Again, education in Africa is planned, financed, and directed by Europeans who as a rule are working for definite practical ends. At the same time the average practical European engaged in organizing or carrying out African teaching is neither an ethnographer nor yet a sociologist. He is as a rule unaware of the wider cultural, social, and political implications of the educational process. Above all, he has usually not studied the African indigenous systems of education. The result is that we often produce educated Africans who have no place in either the tribal world or the European community. It is the duty of the contact anthropologist to study this question within its widest context and its implications. To divorce here the practical implications from theoretical issues would be as difficult as it would be unprofitable.

I trust that throughout the foregoing argument the complete convergence of practical interests on the one hand and those of functional anthropology on the other has become more and more evident. Both concentrate on the same subject matter: demography and law; tribal authority and land tenure; the understanding of family life, sexual morals, and of kinship groupings as local and coöperative factors. All these are obviously as important to the administrator as they are interesting to the functional anthropologist. The educationalist will find that the whole argument of a functional analysis is closely concerned with the problem of how culture is transmitted from generation to generation. The missionary will find that the study of religion as an integrative principle bears directly on his work of evangelization and gradual development of all that is sound, constructive, and real in paganism into higher forms of a Western religion. Thus it is not only the subject matter but the type of interest that remains identical. The functionalist is primarily interested in how institutions work, what they achieve, and how their various factors are related to one another. This in a way also implies the question of how institutions can be transformed. The whole functional approach is based on the principle of the plasticity of human nature and of the possibilities of cultural development. It contains also a warning: the tenacity of custom and the difficulty of transforming the African family into a Christian one, or the indigenous system of administration into something approaching the Western ideal, are explained by the complexity and dovetailing of all human activities. The general rule that slow, gradual, and well-planned transformation can achieve what haphazard, fortuitous muddling through would only confuse is thus a moral to be drawn from the functional analysis of culture. Thus those who have the practical control of African tribes may make almost direct use of the methods of functional field work. For these methods bring them directly to the knowledge of how the political constitution of a tribe is founded and how it works; how Native systems of education proceed and how religion exercises a social and moral influence over its believers.

The Nature of Culture Change

Culture change is a difficult subject to handle and control both in regard to theory and method. We are faced with problems of *whither,* as well as of *whence*. We are dealing with a subject matter which is in flux; the rapidity of change confuses observation and confounds policies. The growth of new unexpected forces and factors, such as African nationalism and the development of autonomous African churches, poses difficulties of description and analysis as well as of policy. In this new work the theoretician and the practitioner must take account of wide issues of Western rule, economic as well as imperial; they have to be acquainted with the rudiments at least of economic, legal, and political theory and, with all this, of anthropological method.

Bearing in mind that we are studying the process of diffusion in empirical field work, and that practical and theoretical interests must be well balanced, our task is to define the nature of the process, the principles and concepts to be used; the method of field work, and the best manner of coöperation between the White agents of change and the theoretical students. A glance at any part of British East or South Africa shows that we have to do, not with one culture, unified or mixed, but with a patchwork of culture areas. These can be classed into three categories, each containing a special type of human life, a special phase of the cultural process. There are districts predominantly European and controlled by Western modes of life and thought. There exist tribal reserves almost purely African. But besides these there are also districts and institutions in which Africans and Europeans collaborate and depend on each other in the most direct and specific manner.

A Bird's-Eye View of Africa Today

In order to make our arguments concrete, let us glance at what Africa looks like today.[4] A passenger flying over the inland route of the Imperial Airways can obtain what is almost literally a bird's-eye view of the cultural situation. After you have followed the green ribbon of the Nile, the landmark of one of the world's oldest civilizations, running up toward the heart of the continent, you receive the first impression of Black Africa in the swamps of the Upper Nile. The circular villages built on the old pattern without a single touch of European architecture; the Natives in their old clothes—or lack of them—moving among the cattle penned in the inner enclosure; the obvious isolation of each settlement in what appear to be almost inaccessible swamps

4. This section, "A Bird's-Eye View of Africa Today" (pp. 9–11), is quoted substantially as it appears in Malinowski's introductory essay on "The Anthropology of Changing African Cultures," reprinted from *Methods of Study of Culture Contact in Africa*, Memorandum XV, The International Institute of African Languages and Cultures (1938), pp. vii–x. Ed.

—all this gives at least a surface effect of old untouched Africa. And there is no doubt that we still have here one of the extensive strongholds of indigenous culture.

As soon as the plane crosses the border between Nilotic and Bantu peoples, it becomes obvious that it is a transformed Africa over which we are moving. Among the Baganda the houses are new, square, built on the European pattern; even from above, the dress and ornaments of the Natives spell Manchester and Birmingham. Roads and churches, motor cars and lorries, proclaim that we are in a world of change in which two factors are working together and producing a new type of culture, related both to Europe and Africa, yet not a mere copy of either. When the plane descends in Kisumu we are in a small town largely controlled by the gold-mining interests of the region. Part of it looks almost European. Some streets remind us of India. But the whole is a compound product with an existence of its own, determined by the proximity of several African tribes, by the activities of the Europeans who live and trade there, and the fact of Indian immigration. It is an important center of gold export and trade; as such, it must be studied by the sociologist in relation to world markets, overseas industrial centers and banking organizations, as well as to African labor and natural resources.

In Nairobi we enter a world where Natives and things African seem to play but the role of mutes and properties respectively. The place is dominated by large European administrative buildings, banks, churches, and stores. The White inhabitants go about their European business and live in a world almost untouched, on its surface, by Africa. In reality it rests on African foundations. It would be a grave sociological misconception to take the favorite local slogan, the description of the East African Highlands as "White Man's Country," in its full and literal meaning. The European culture of East Africa, though largely imported from Europe, has become adapted to the African physical environment and remains dependent on the African human milieu.

We meet this tripartite division—old Africa, imported Europe, and the new composite culture—all along the route of plane, railway, and motor road. You come upon Native reserves, where you can still listen to African music, watch African dances, see African ceremonies, speak to Africans dressed in their old attire, ignorant of any European language, and living almost completely their old tribal life.

And then not far away, in a settler's bungalow or in a small European community, you listen to music from England on the short wave, and enjoy "purely European" songs all about "Alabama" and the "Baby" and the "Coon crooning with the crickets"; you can read the latest *Tatler* or *Sketch*, and enjoy a discussion on sport, local or overseas, or English party politics. This world the African enters only as a shadowy figure: the servant bringing the tray with "sundowner" drinks; snatches of African songs drifting in from the plantation compound. Otherwise, the European lives in complete oblivion of indigenous African life. A funny anecdote now and then; questions of labor, administrative queries, or missionary difficulties are at times discussed by those professionally concerned with the control of one or the other indigenous problems. But this does not lead to a full interest in Native life for its own sake.

The color bar in the social and cultural, as well as in the economic sense, largely determines the relations between Europeans and Africans. To regard these relations either as a "well-integrated area of common existence" or as a simple "mixture" based on direct "borrowing" ignores the real driving forces of the impact and reaction and takes no count of the strong mutual resistances and antagonisms of the two races and cultures.

Yet there is give and take. There is live contact and coöperation. There are activities where Europeans must rely on African labor, and Africans are at times willing to serve, or can be induced into signing a contract. There are processes and events in which whole groups of Europeans spontaneously and generously offer what they regard as best in European culture to the Africans. The Africans, again, appreciating the value and the advantages of European religion, education, and technology—or startled by the novelty thereof—begin often by adopting Western ways eagerly and wholeheartedly. Quite as often they end by reacting in movements completely uncontrolled and uncontrollable by the missionary or administrator, and at times directly hostile to the Whites.

Everywhere in Africa we now meet places and institutions where culture contact is made as in a workshop. Education is given in schools and evangelizing is carried on in churches and mission stations. A mixture of customary and alien law is administered in Native courts supervised by Europeans; or again by European magistrates more or less acquainted with Native codes and customs.

Thus even from a purely superficial survey we can conclude that changing Africa is not a single subject matter but one composed of three phases. It would almost be possible to take a piece of chalk and on the face of the continent to map out spatially the areas of each type: predominantly European, genuinely African, and those covered by the processes of change.[5]

5. End of quotation from "A Bird's-Eye View of Africa Today."

Each phase—European, African, and that of culture contact and change—is subject to its own specific cultural determinism. The White inmates of a town, mission station, a settler's homestead, or administrative compound remain in touch with the mother country. Their educational ideals, their religious faith, their political allegiances, their scientific or economic interests, are one and all European, based on European training, depending on European institutions, and often directly guided from Europe.

The reserves of African tribalism draw their strength from local indigenous tradition. Their adaptation to their environment is the result of an age-long process. They are politically controlled by chiefs or councils to whom they owe an allegiance based on African ideas, beliefs, and sentiments. Even when the tribesmen are converted to an alien religion, educated in European schools, and submitted to European rule and jurisdiction, they still retain many of their own views and sentiments, the product of African culture and the African environment.

When we come to institutions which are the result of contact and change, we find again that they are neither completely moved by European influences nor yet by African, but obey a specific determinism of their own.

All this imposes new tasks on modern anthropology, in that it must henceforth concern itself with culture change. The student has to understand in what the processes of culture change consist. He must be aware of what the essential factors are: such for instance as the European influences, the resistance of Native cultures to change, the eagerness to adopt some of the new methods while rejecting others—in short, the forces and factors of transformation. The fieldworker has to devise means of studying these phenomena; of organizing them and presenting them in a clear and convincing manner. Change is obviously more difficult to study than stable and well-crystallized conditions. In working on the problem we need some fixed frame of reference to which the multiplicity of factors, the protean variety of things in flux, can be related. A correct theory of change must, therefore, yield methods of empirical research. Finally, as has been urged already, the anthropologist has to make himself useful. He is a member of the active Western civilization which has started, and to a large extent, still controls the processes of contact. It is the duty of his science to contribute as much information and advice as possible to the controlling agents of change.

Let us then consider the three following points:

1. The nature of culture change.
2. Empirical methods of field work best suited to give a clear picture of culture change in each particular case.
3. The principles of practical advice, founded on that power of foresight which all sound science is bound to supply; criteria of adaptability and vitality of African institutions; and the possibility of forecasts in the process of culture change.[6]

6. In Memorandum XV of the International Institute of African Languages and Cultures, a series of articles on culture change was published in 1938 under the title of *Methods of Study of Culture Contact in Africa*. Many of the writers contributed answers, implied or explicit, to the problems posed above. Since their material is drawn from our field of study, Africa, and since many of their theories and methods are those held by anthropologists in other parts of the world, I shall take up in the following chapter some of the points which they raise for the study of culture change.

II

THEORIES OF CULTURE CHANGE

The Contact Situation as an Integral Whole

As regards the nature of culture change, one simple solution occurs immediately. A contact situation is at any moment a cultural reality. Why should we not regard it as an "integral whole," since in any particular case we have Africans and Englishmen, Indians and Mediterranean immigrants working together within the same habitat on joint cultural tasks? Once we make this assumption the problem of empirical field work solves itself. We should have to use the same methods and devices which the old anthropologist used in the study of his primitive, relatively unaffected, single culture.

It is now generally agreed upon that Europeans form an integral part of any contact situation. Some time ago I somewhat flippantly urged that "an enlightened anthropologist has to take account of European stupidity and prejudice" quite as fully as of African superstition and backwardness.[1] I would now reframe it more soberly in claiming that the whole range of European influences, interests, good intentions, and predatory drives must become an essential part of the study of African culture change. This point of view, indeed, has now become almost a commonplace of field work and theory. But I think it is pushing a legitimate commonplace too far when it is suggested that "the missionary, administrator, trader and labour recruiter must be regarded as factors in the tribal life in the same way as are the chief and the magician." [2] And as regards field work, we are advised that "there is no special technique required for investigations of this kind . . ." Yet another writer has claimed: "Contact agents can be treated as integrally part of the community." [3] This sounds plausible

1. Malinowski, "Practical Anthropology," *Africa*, Vol. VII (1929).
2. I. Schapera, "Contact between European and Native in South Africa—2: In Bechuanaland," *Methods of Study of Culture Contact in Africa*, p. 27.
3. *Vide* M. Fortes, "Culture Contact as a Dynamic Process," *Methods of Study of Culture Contact in Africa*, p. 62.
Malinowski's criticism of this position would also apply to that adopted by Dr. Gluckman in an article entitled "Analysis of a Social Situation in Modern Zululand," in *Bantu Studies*, Vol. XIV (1940). Dr. Gluckman there states: "We see that the dominant form of the structure is the existence *within a single community* [my italics] of two co-operating colour groups which are differentiated by a large number of criteria so as to stand opposed and even hostile to one another" (p. 28). Dr. Gluckman admits the existence of a color bar; unfortunately, he does not define the term com-

and would certainly make matters very simple. We should have only a slight numerical addition to our informants and perhaps an improvement in their quality. We could regard local Europeans as expert sources of information and employ them for this purpose in the same way as one would use Native informants.[4]

Unfortunately, this type of simplification is not advisable. The treatment of the complex situations of change as one "well integrated whole," the "one-entry" approach as we might call it, ignores the whole dynamism of the process. It takes no account of the main fact in culture change, that is, that European residents, the missionaries and the administrators, the settlers and the entrepreneurs, are indeed the main agents of change. The concept of a well-integrated community would, indeed, ignore such facts as the color bar, the permanent rift which divides the two partners in change and keeps them apart in church and factory, in matters of mine labor and political influence.

Above all, it obscures and distorts the only correct conception of culture change in such areas: the fact that it is the result of an impact of a higher, active culture upon a simpler, more passive one. The typical phenomena of change, the adoption or rejection, the transformation of certain institutions and the growth of new ones, are ruled out by the concept of a well-integrated community or culture.

This concept, however, expresses the partial and minor truth: a small community, stationary or stagnant, or one which has been hardly affected as yet by the full impact of westernization, can be regarded as being in a state of temporary adjustment. The missionary has converted part of the tribe while the rest remain heathen. The administrator may not have opportunities or motives for encroaching on the old tribal life. The trader established some time ago may be furnishing the goods which have already become indispensable, and receives in return money or Native produce. This group of people who cooperate, who live side by side for the time being in relations which have little of the "dynamic" in them; who are temporarily adjusted to each other—this can be studied as an integral whole.

What assumption, however, were we compelled to make in order to achieve this temporarily useful simplification? We agreed for the moment to forget the fact of change. This obviously is illegitimate when change is the main subject of our study. Just when we are trying

munity. If, however, we take it to mean a territorial group which participates in a common culture, it is difficult to see how it can be applied to the African contact situation, in view of the profound differences of language and culture between the two groups involved. Ed.

4. *Vide* Schapera, *op. cit.*, p. 28, for this suggestion.

to organize our work and interests round the *concept of change* and methods of field work for the study of culture contact, it is not admissible to forget that European agents constitute everywhere the main drive in change; that they are the determining factors as regards the initiative of change; that it is they who plan, take measures, and import things into Africa; that they withhold; that they take away land, labor, and political independence; and that they themselves are in most of their actions determined by instructions, ideas, and forces which have their origin outside Africa.

Take the missionary.[5] He cannot "be regarded in the same way as the magician . . ." The missionary is the initiator and center of the religious revolution now taking place in Africa. He would not be true to his vocation if he ever agreed to act on the principle that Christianity is as "any other form of cult." As a matter of fact, his brief is to regard all the other forms of religion as misguided, fit only for destruction, and to regard Christianity as entirely different, the only true religion to be implanted. Far from leaving other cults side by side in juxtaposition with the message of the Gospels, the missionary is actively engaged in superseding them.

The administrator, again, far from ever becoming an equivalent of the old chief, far from representing tribal authority in any sense of being an integral part of it, must always remain over and above the tribe, and must control from without. He is not regarded as the chief, because he does not act as such. The average British official tries to administer justice and to be a father of his wards. But is he from his point of view an integral part of the tribe? No. He was neither born nor bred to it, nor is he very conversant with any of its ideas; he is, in fact, a servant of the British Empire, temporarily working in such and such a colony, a public school boy, an Englishman, or a Scotsman. He has to safeguard the interests of the empire first and foremost. He has to watch over European interests in the colony, as well as to maintain the balance of these interests as against native claims. To conceive of the part played by European political agents in Africa in terms of a fictitious "well-integrated" community would blind us to the very definition of the tasks, nature, and implications of colonial administration.

Nor can industrial enterprise be regarded as part of a tribal unit. It would be a strange African tribe which would embrace the gold mines of the Rand, with their gigantic plant; the stock exchange of Johannes-

5. The following discussion of European agents considered as part of an African tribe is taken from Malinowski's "The Anthropology of Changing African Cultures," *Methods of Study of Culture Contact in Africa*, pp. xv–xvii; but I have also inserted sections from his other manuscripts. Ed.

burg, and the banking system stretching from Cape to Cairo. The communication systems, railroads, and planes of the Imperial Airways, the system of motor roads with the cars and lorries which run on them —all this is part of culture contact. But the concept of an extended African tribe, into which this could be squeezed in order to produce a unified tribal horizon, falls to the ground as soon as it is stated.[6]

It would be equally difficult to regard the settler and his African neighbor as brethren of a large family; quite as difficult as to apply this concept to some of the Afrikaans-speaking groups and to the Kaffirs, the integration with whom runs against the fundamental principles of the *Grondwet,* or constitution of the Boer Republics.

As regards the possibility of practical applications, the conception of culture change as the impact of Western civilization and the reaction thereto of indigenous cultures is the only fruitful approach. We must treat the plans, intentions, and interests of White contact agents as something which can only be realized through coöperation with the African; or which fails because of real conflict of interests, faulty planning, misunderstanding, or lack of a common ground for effective joint work. Here the anthropologist can act as adviser only if he realizes clearly that at times there is a possibility of effective coöperation; that there are definite conditions under which this is possible, while in certain cases an inevitable clash must result.[7]

The subject matter of culture change differs then from that of stationary cultures, studied by ordinary anthropological field work, in several respects. There are the impinging culture and the one which receives. There are, therefore, two cultures to deal with instead of one; the modifications wrought on the recipients by the aggressors, and also *vice versa.* Not only that. There is always the formation of an aggressive or conquering community *in situ* (i.e., White settlers). This community is by no means a direct replica of its mother com-

6. End of quotation from Malinowski's "The Anthropology of Changing African Cultures." Ed.

7. I should like to add that Professor Schapera in his article puts on the map of ethnographic work the study of "the various motives and interests which have driven each of these agencies to encroach upon the natives" (*vide op. cit.,* p. 33). But the manner in which he would like to lay the foundations for field work, as stated in his essay under the subheading "Basic Investigations" (pp. 27 ff.) is not quite compatible with his more correct subsequent statement of the problem.

There is one more argument from the contribution of Professor Schapera I would like to challenge. His insistence on "personalities" as opposed to "institutions" is puzzling. It leads him to the assertion: "to the native . . . there is no such thing as Western civilization in general" (*op. cit.,* p. 34). But is not the essence of tribal reaction to White contact, of Bantu nationalism, and of the various Pan-African movements, a public opinion in which the Western world as a whole is made the object of violent views and strong sentiments?

munity at home. The interaction between Native and European communities offers opportunities for the introduction of third parties, such as Indians, Syrians, and Arabs in Africa; at times, the growth of a mixed population, such as Cape Colored in South Africa. All this complicates the problem immensely, or rather, multiplies the constituent parts of the subject matter.

The anthropologist here cannot study any more a well-defined, circumscribed entity like an Oceanic island. He deals with a segment of a vast continent,[8] with a community surrounded by an enormous hinterland. In reality, he has two such hinterlands to deal with in an ethnological sense: one of them the hinterland of European culture with which the White community are in contact, by which they are directed, from which they constantly import goods and receive ideas, and into which in one way or another they will ultimately return. The African has also his hinterland, his old culture, now a thing of the past; and in another sense, his own community to which he has to return after his short excursions into White contact; and more than that, the hinterland of other tribes with whom he will have to cooperate.

If the ordinary anthropology is therefore a matter of one-column entries, that of culture change will have at least three: White hinterland, Black hinterland, and the column of culture contact. No phenomenon in the middle column of contacts can be studied without constant reference to both White and Native sides.

Diffusion

If we were to look for a ready solution in existing ethnological theory for the handling of evidence on culture change, we should naturally turn to that doctrine of diffusion and historical relations of past cultures elaborated by the school of which Ratzel is the ancestor, but to which many German and American anthropologists have made notable contributions. These schools conceive of diffusion as a migration of elements or traits from one culture to another. They are supposed to be adopted in solution or compounded into complexes, of which the component elements are not naturally related to one another. The product of diffusion is thus conceived of as a mixture of cultural elements or of complexes, so loosely knit together that the main theoretical task of cultural analysis into cultural strata or other

8. Dr. Audrey I. Richards in "The Village Census in the Study of Culture Contact," *Methods of Study of Culture Contact in Africa*, p. 46, also makes a similar point, and suggests that this will modify the guiding principles of field work from the start.

heterogeneous units consists in disentangling them from their matrix and showing whence they came.

Thus fortuitous comparative studies between Melanesian and West African cultures claim to have established that the bow-and-arrow culture has migrated from its home somewhere in Melanesia, over to West Africa and to other parts of the world. Other studies have shown the historical influence of large currents of culture radiating from Southeast Asia through the Sunda Archipelago into Oceania. The British School of Diffusionism has in its inspiring reconstructive work sought to establish the proof that the archaic culture of Egypt left its mark throughout the world in a gradual progress across the ancient Orient—India, China, the islands of the Pacific, and over to the New World.

Valuable and suggestive as such studies are, the methods on which they are based and their central concepts will have to be overhauled from top to bottom in the light of the new empirical material derived from actual field work on present-day diffusion, especially as it happens in Africa. Anticipating some of the subsequent results, I should say, for instance, that Graebner's criteria of identity, the well-known principle of criteria of form and quantity, and of unrelated traits will have to be dropped. In fact the treatment of diffusion in terms of trait and trait complexes seems to me of doubtful value.[9] The empirical study of diffusion reveals to us that the process is not one of indiscriminate give and accidental take but is directed by definite forces and pressures on the side of the donor culture and well-determined resistances on the part of the recipients. We shall find also that diffusion cannot be studied at all in field work unless we realize that the units of transformation are not traits or trait complexes but organized systems or institutions. It is the European administration which influences Native tribal authority; it is Western enterprise which modifies African labor; and it is the organized missionary society which transforms an organized African religion.

9. Malinowski in "The Present State of Studies in Culture Contact: Some Comments on an American Approach," *Africa*, XII (1939), p. 31, again makes a similar criticism in discussing the point of view of Herskovits: "The breaking up of a culture into component 'traits' and its reassembling into 'trait complexes' is not compatible with the scientific analysis of culture into real units of organized interests and activities. The only attempt at a full and explicit definition of 'traits' so far given is that of Graebner, which has been fully accepted and endorsed by Pater Schmidt, by Wissler, and by Kroeber. It is based on the identification of irrelevant form and fortuitous concatenation—an identification of cultural factors which the functionalist will never be able to accept." For a more detailed criticism of diffusion, see also Malinowski's article "Anthropology," *Encyclopaedia Britannica* (13th ed. 1926). Ed.

The Product of Change as a Mixture of Elements

Another conception of the phenomena of change largely follows the theoretical principles implied in the school of German and American diffusionists. This view eschews the mistake of regarding change as an integrated cultural phenomenon, and correctly recognizes that as we find it now African culture is not a homogeneous one. Dr. Monica Hunter among British anthropologists is perhaps the most outspoken advocate of a special approach to culture problems and the need of new methods for culture change. Following, however, the diffusionists' ideas and methods of "cultural analysis," she conceives of the term "mixture" in a somewhat mechanical manner. In her opinion, the main task of anthropology would be "as far as possible to distinguish elements borrowed from European culture from those which were a part of Pondo culture before the coming of Europeans." [10]

She explicitly opposes the "purely functional study" to the "contact study," and she is keenly aware that the point of view of the strict functionalist must be modified when we approach a rapidly changing African civilization and the impact of European influences. The reader of the previous arguments will see that I am in full agreement with the need of developing new methods, new instruments of presentation, and of widening the scope of antiquarian anthropology. The three-column approach is one which was not necessary to the older type of field work, concerned only with a stationary Native community. But it will be clear that I cannot agree with the statement that the culture is a "mixture of partially fused elements which can only be understood in terms of the parent cultures"; [11] or again, when she speaks of the "impossibility of understanding existing institutions without a knowledge of the past." [12]

The passages quoted invite us to examine several questions, for they are extremely pertinent for the formulation of methods of study and of a theory of culture change. Does the simile of a "mixture of partially fused elements" suggest a correct vision of the nature of culture change? Do we really have to deal with a mechanical juxtaposition or jumble, with elements lifted out of two contexts and mixed in different proportions? Again, in what sense can a present phase of development and change be understood in terms of parent cultures? Are

10. Monica Hunter, "Contact between European and Native in South Africa—1: In Pondoland," *Methods of Study of Culture Contact in Africa*, p. 18.
  Dr. Elsie Clews Parsons in her book *Mitla* (1936) also followed a similar process of sorting out indigenous and Spanish elements in Zapotecan culture. Ed.
11. Hunter, *op. cit.*, p. 10.
12. *Ibid.*

changes in Africa directly related to European culture on the one hand and to old African culture on the other? In reality, is not the European in Africa something profoundly different from the European at home? By this I mean that the impact of European interests, influences, and active agencies is not a mere fusion or mixing but something orientated on different lines with definite purposes, which are not quite integrated with each other, and which therefore do not act in any simple manner; above all, do not simply mix or fuse with African cultures but modify them in a much more complicated and dynamic way.[13]

We could, of course, by ferreting round in any urban location, mine compound, or even Native reserve, draw up a list of objects, customs, and activities which to the superficial observer would naturally fall into their respective European and African categories.

In a single visit to the oldest and most dilapidated of the Native yards in Johannesburg, I registered the following assortment: a divining performance carried out by a Zulu witch doctor; a Methodist prayer meeting with hymns and preaching complete; young lads preparing for an initiation ceremony; an African "board and pebble game" played for European money; and the following collection of objects: boots from a Moravian factory, a bicycle from Japan, an assortment of dress objects coming from Indian, English, German, and American tailors.

Each article and each activity could easily be invoiced back to its place of origin. Some came obviously from abroad. Others—the game, the divination, a few ornaments, trinkets, and articles in the diviner's dress—were African. So also was the assortment of medical substances, snakes, bats, and baboons' skulls, which were displayed for sale. The insistence on the range and heterogeneity of origin panders to our delight in the incongruousness of the weird collection. Yet such a mechanical invoicing back misses completely the significance of the whole process which brought the Native yard into being, with all that is and happens there.

Take any object, for instance, the Japanese bicycle. These extremely low-priced articles are made especially for the African market. As such, they are not part of the Japanese culture, not even of the modern one. The demand for them is the result of all the complex forces which make the Native desire assimilation for its own sake because of European prestige and the halo of superiority. Again, the use of the bicycle is made possible by European activities, such as the establishment

13. The following paragraphs (pp. 21–22) are taken with minor alterations from Malinowski's "Modern Anthropology and European Rule in Africa." Reale Accademia d'Italia, Fondazione Alessandro Volta, Estratto dagli Atti dell' VIII Convegno (Rome, 1938; published 1940), XVIII, 17–19. Ed.

of roads and communications, and the African necessity for quick and easy transport from his place of living to the place of work. The African in some areas is not admitted to buses, or trams, so has to use the bicycle.

Thus neither the African demand nor yet the mechanisms of supply can be understood unless we consider this single item against the background of the complex but clearly defined forces of impact.

Take the articles of dress. The Native who serves as a constable or as a soldier, who contracts for mine work, or domestic employment, is often directly uniformed, while as a convert he has to assume the garb of Christian respectability. None of these uniforms is copied from the European pattern, or yet from the African. The Johannesburg financier who employs a cook or house boy does not try to assimilate him to his own appearance, or even to that of a butler or valet, but puts him directly into the attire of an African servant.

Thus the adoption of European dress is not the taking over of "isolated traits" but the result of organized processes. If we want to understand it, we have to consider European trade, European employment agencies, as well as the whole psychology which works in institutions, in the submission to European prestige and superiority, and in the definite programs for the partial metamorphoses of the African.

What is clear about material objects receives even deeper significance when we come to social phenomena and manifestations of spiritual culture. Divination and witchcraft found in a town yard are not mere replicas of the genuine African institutions. The performance I saw in Johannesburg was African divination, but it was applied to a case of witchcraft turning around the competitions and jealousies of mine employment; the fee was paid in English money, and the verdict was given in terms which no tribesman would understand. The initiation ceremonies carried out round Johannesburg are a symptom of a return to certain tribal values, profoundly changed in the process. Thus again, any attempt at a deeper understanding leads us far away from playing about with "traits," "trait complexes," or "cultural strata." [14]

The problems here raised are interesting and important, both for anthropological theory in general and for the field with which we are concerned, that of the principles and methods of culture change. Let us therefore carry our analysis further by examining some of the other institutions in which Europeans and Africans are involved. [15]

14. End of citation from "Modern Anthropology and European Rule in Africa."
15. The following section (pp. 23-26) is taken from Malinowski's "The Anthropology of Changing African Cultures," *Methods of Study of Culture Contact in Africa*, pp. xix-xxii. Additional material has however been inserted from his other manuscripts. Ed.

Take such a typical product of change such as a big industrial enterprise—an African gold or copper mine. Can we envisage it in terms of mixture, a juxtaposition or assortment of "partially fused elements" from Europe and Africa? Obviously not. It is a new type of enterprise, organized by Western capital and European initiative but working in exotic surroundings and with African labor. Imagine an assortment of elements "borrowed" from the Western civilization: the mining plant—the tools, trucks, and rails; the machinery for pounding the ore; the various engineering appliances—all dumped on the veldt or in the jungle. Imagine whole regiments of African labor driven toward it, as well as a contingent of skilled European workmen and engineers planted there. All this juxtaposed, mechanically put together, does not yet constitute a mine or a factory. It can only be regarded as a set of conditions necessary but not sufficient for the creation of this industry. Where "borrowing" ends, culture change begins. The translation of financial and engineering plans into an organization of African labor for the exploitation of African resources is a new process, a genuine process of contact and change.

Once the new industrial venture is organized, we have a complicated European enterprise, essentially dependent on African labor and resources, a phenomenon which can no more be dissected into bits African and European. It cannot be understood either as a whole, or yet in any of its component parts, in terms of European or African prototypes. There is no European prototype for color-bar legislation or practice; for recruiting on reserves; for the method of unemployment insurance by throwing back superfluous labor onto the tribal areas in times of slump. The remuneration of labor, based on the differential discrimination between the races, the type of contract with unilateral criminal sanctions current in Africa, the inducements to sign on—all this is new to both Europe and Africa. It is determined by the fact that we have two races and two cultures influencing each other. The concept of the mechanical incorporation of elements from one culture into another does not lead us beyond the initial preparatory stages, and even then on subtler analysis breaks down. What really takes place is an interplay of specific contact forces: race prejudice, political and economic imperialism, the demand for segregation, the safeguarding of a European standard of living, and the African reaction to all this. To approach any one of the large autonomous industrial enterprises in Africa with the conception of a "mixture" would lead us to give up the study of the process at the very point where it really becomes significant.

African labor differs from European labor legally, economically, and socially. At the same time this labor cannot be related in any way to African tribal economics. The scale of payment, criminal sanctions for contracts, pass laws, and diet problems which occur in South Africa cannot be understood in terms of the European or of the African parent cultures.[16] No sorting of elements is possible; no invoicing back to a previous culture as an element of reality. For we have here to deal with a vast phenomenon which in its essence is defined by a set of economic, legal, and social arrangements which have arisen in response to a new need: the large-scale exploitation of African resources by Europeans, for Western ends and by means of African labor. The fallacy of regarding such a phenomenon as a heap of fragments "borrowed" from Black and White parent cultures is evident.

The task of the fieldworker cannot consist in disengaging and reassorting the Black and White elements of the imaginary conglomerate, for the reality of culture change is not a conglomerate, nor a mixture, nor yet a juxtaposition of partially fused elements.

Take another example. The slum yards of Johannesburg, themselves a product of culture contact, would supply us with yet another "mixture"—one symptomatic and symbolic of culture change—*skokian*, the famous concoction brewed, retailed, and consumed in the notorious slum yards of Native South African locations. The modern girl looking for a shocker for her cocktail party may find a recipe in the Report of the Native Economic Commission.[17] "Appallingly noxious drinks were invented. Anything which quickly increased the alcoholic content was added; calcium carbide, methylated spirits, tobacco, molasses and sugar, blue stone, are only a few examples." The ingredients of this mixture have never figured in any mixed drinks party in Bloomsbury or Greenwich Village. As elements of a "cocktail" they were not "borrowed" but readapted by African genius to a new function. And obviously the African parent culture supplies no "precedents" for any use of calcium carbide, blue stone, or methylated spirits. Skokian is a legitimate offspring of the slum yard by European moral intentions. Read the accompanying paragraphs in the report, and you will find that skokian arose in response to "the problem . . . of inventing a drink which could be made and stored in small quantities, easy to hide, which could be matured in a few hours, and could have its alcoholic effect quickly." For in the general puritanic drive against Native beer—itself an entirely innocuous drink—and the police control by which it was enforced, the Native was driven to invent skokian and its peers.

16. For details of pass laws, penal sanctions, and usages in Africa, see Lord Hailey's *An African Survey*, pp. 659–672, 682–685.

17. Report of the Native Economic Commission, 1930–32, U.G. 22, 1932; p. 110, par. 751.

Are such phenomena as Native townships or mining compounds, African small holdings or agricultural coöperatives, a mixture? Hardly. They are one and all entirely new products of conditions which are the outgrowth of the impact of European civilization on archaic Africa. Again, when we observe the cases where in African villages there have been adopted very much simplified types of European houses, we find that with these there goes invariably a whole set of prerequisites and concomitant conditions. Those who adopt European housing are the educated and Christianized Natives, trained in habits of rudimentary hygiene and cleanliness, employed by Whites or raising European cash crops. For a certain amount of ready cash is necessary in order to construct, maintain, and use this new material object. Indeed, an empirical research into the problem would show that it is not a house or a bedstead which is adopted, nor yet a cultural complex, consisting of all these objects, but rather an integral institution of westernized family life; based on Christianity and education; on the adoption of certain European pursuits, and the use of money. But even this is a metaphorical way of speaking. What actually happens is the formation all over Africa of a new type of indigenous domesticity, the result of certain specified European influences which, however, in the act of being taken over by the Africans, have been profoundly modified.

The school in the Bush has no antecedents in Europe or in African tribalism. The question of educating men and women to professions from the practice of which they are then legally debarred occurs neither in Europe nor yet in Bantu Africa. Take the educated African as a final product of the process. I would like to meet the ethnographer who could accomplish the task of sorting out a westernized African into his component parts without destroying the one thing in him which matters—his personality. The educated African is a new type of human being, endowed with abilities and energies, with advantages and handicaps, with problems and visions, which neither his European neighbor nor his "blanket" brother are heirs to.

The nature of culture change is determined by factors and circumstances which cannot be assessed by the study of either culture alone, or of both of them as lumber rooms of elements. The clash and interplay of the two cultures produce new things. Even a material object, a tool or an instrument like money, changes in the very process of culture contact. The anthropologist has to correlate European good intentions with the necessities of the situation; the inspired liberalism and good-will of the missionary with the more materialistic designs of the financier, entrepreneur, and settler. The whole concept of European culture as a cornucopia from which things are freely given is misleading.[18] The European takes as much, in fact a great deal more, than he gives. But what he takes away are not cultural traits but land, wealth, and labor. This is not an indictment nor a piece of pro-Native ranting. It is simply a strong *caveat* that an approach which eliminates from the study of change the real driving forces is insufficient.

It is necessary, I think, to make plain once and for all that to treat the process of culture change as a static product, in which Europeans and Africans have arrived at a system of temporary integration or of harmonized unity, is unprofitable. Equally unprofitable is it to treat the process as a mechanical mixture where the main problem consists in the sorting out and invoicing back of elements. The phenomena of change are new cultural realities, which have to be studied directly with the full consciousness that we have to deal here with at least three phases; that these three phases interact; but that their interaction cannot be anticipated by an assessment of the original ingredients.

The study of culture change must take into account three orders of reality: the impact of the higher culture; the substance of Native life on which it is directed; and the phenomenon of autonomous change resulting from the reaction between the two cultures. Only by analyzing each problem under these three headings, and then confronting the column of European influences with that of Native responses, and of the resulting change, do we arrive at the most useful instruments of research. Far from being a mere mechanical joining of the two original influences, European and African, the two impinge on each other. The impact produces conflict, coöperation, or leads to compromise.

18. End of quotation from "The Anthropology of Changing African Cultures."

III

THE VALUE OF HISTORY AND ITS LIMITATIONS

The Search for the Zero Point of Change

ONE more view taken as to the nature of contact phenomena must be scrutinized: that which regards change as a deviation from the original conditions of equilibrium and adjustment, almost as a fall from the grace of original tribalism. Change also generally implies maladjustment, deterioration, social strain, and confusion in legal and moral principles. Is it not therefore natural to assume that culture change is essentially an aberration from normal conditions? Dr. Mair has introduced the apposite expression, "zero point" of culture change, to designate the conditions of pre-European tribal equilibrium.

This view is both plausible and tempting. In order to account for the degree and the "causes" of change, it seems inevitable and necessary to turn to its starting point. The memories of your old informants, especially trustworthy in all matters of tribal lore, depict the old times as the Golden Age of human existence. The natural bias of every ethnographer leads him also to regard the untainted Native culture not merely as the *terminus ab quo* but as the *terminus ad quem* of normalcy, as the only legitimate standard of comparison between the pathology of change and the healthy condition of tribalism. Indeed, all scientific work demands a fixed system of coördinates, a definite set of bearings, and the zero point of contact and change seems at first sight to offer the best framework for the assessment of any deviation from the normal. Such comparison would then provide, in the words of Dr. Mair, "an objective basis for the determination of policy." [1]

Dr. Mair, in her able exposition of this approach, insists that the discovery of such maladjustments in present-day African institutions requires as a starting point a reconstruction of the working of these institutions in precontact times.[2] Although she admits the limitations of such reconstruction, she defends the historical approach as essential for the analysis of the contact situation. In defending her attitude, she distinguishes between more or less static societies and those undergoing rapid changes; and maintains that in a static society, where institutions have become firmly established and stabilized, the knowl-

1. Lucy P. Mair, "The Place of History in the Study of Culture Contact," *Methods of Study of Culture Contact in Africa*, p. 8.
2. *Idem*, p. 2.

edge of the past would be immaterial for a functional understanding of the present. But in a changing society, where innovations have not yet crystallized into their place, where the subsidiary modifications in the social structure have not yet been made, the contrast of past with present is of great significance.[3] This distinction by Dr. Mair of static and dynamic phases in the history of a culture and the suggestion of two different methods, the functional and the historical, for the study of these different phases have far-reaching theoretical implications. They would mean that the functional method is limited in its exclusive applicability to the study of a stable, balanced culture, in which all systems of social coöperation are in a state of equilibrium.

Dr. Mair carries the distinction between the static and the dynamic phase of a culture to the point of saying that the well-adjusted and therefore static phase is the normal state of a culture, while the dynamic phase, which we encounter under present-day conditions of manifold contacts, presents a pathological condition. Such a dual conception of culture, if it is to mean a difference in principle and not merely in degree, is a working hypothesis which must be tested carefully before it can be made the basis of a discussion on methodology.

In discussing the exact nature of the historical comparison of the traditional culture and the contact situation, Dr. Mair denies the sociological significance of a study of intermediate stages, because it is no longer possible to correlate the various historical events with the development of the Native culture at the time each of these events took place.[4] Therefore, she concludes that all the anthropologist could do and should do in the study of culture contact is to compare the traditional Native institutions, i.e., the Native culture at the zero point of contact influences, with the present-day situation.[5]

I have already insisted that reconstruction is and will remain one of the main tasks of scientific ethnology. But to admit the legitimacy of the reconstructive interest, even an antiquarian passion, is one thing; to assume that reconstruction is a specific method for the study of culture contact is another. First of all, it is essential not to confuse the reconstructed past with the reality of what still survives as a vital residue of past history. The fact, for instance, that chieftainship persists where it is completely ignored by European influences proves that this institution is still alive in such areas. Chieftainship of a few generations ago, however, must have been different from the form in which

3. *Idem*, p. 3.
4. *Idem*, p. 6.
5. We have already discussed a similar position adopted by Dr. Hunter on her search for a "common background" (*vide* pp. 13, 14 of her article).

it survives today; for the pre-European situation implied absolute sovereignty—complete and undivided power, the right to carry on war and slave raids and to control the wealth of the tribe. What matters for the future and even for the present is what is still alive and not what is dead.

It is equally important to realize that the "past remembered"—that is, its vision in man's memory—need not, in fact cannot, be reconstructed. It must be studied simply by tapping the memories of the tribesmen. And here we come to another confusion, that between the mythological vision of the past as entertained by the Natives and the sober picture which would emerge from scientific reconstruction. To some Africans who are still true to their own culture, the past becomes in retrospect the Paradise lost forever. To the progressives or the renegades, who often gain substantially by the change, the past is the time of unmitigated evil. To trust to the memories of old men or to current accounts of what used to be would, for the purposes of reconstruction, be futile. To the student of culture change, what really matters is not the objectively true past, scientifically reconstructed and all-important to the antiquarian, but the psychological reality of today. The former is an order of events dead and buried, even to the length of having disappeared from men's memories; the latter is a powerful psychological force determining the present-day behavior of the Native African. People are swayed by the errors of what they feel and not by the truth which they ignore.

Moreover the reconstructed past is not always known with precision, and the anthropologist will very often have to say on the point of reconstruction, *Ignoramus ignorabimus*. Around the Gulf of Guinea where contact began in the times of Henry the Navigator, the task of reconstruction is obviously futile. But even where contact is a hundred years old, or only a few decades, reconstruction may be just as difficult. In the whole of Southeast Africa the revolutionary changes produced by the founding and expansion of the Zulu Empire under Chaka have made the search for pre-European normal conditions of peaceful and integrated tribal life practically impossible. Dr. Hunter, who, as we have seen, believes that "any culture can only be fully understood in its historical context," has nevertheless to admit that throughout Southeast Africa "there are no adequate data on Bantu life as it was before contact with Europeans." [6] She gives also the real reason why the use of a "reconstructed past" in any comparative discussion is useless. If we want to compare the present state of a changing culture with its zero point, we would have to study both by the same methods, and with the same problems in view. "But unfortunately for the student of culture change, the science of social anthropology has been developed since the opening up of Africa." [6]

We are thus faced with this position: at times reconstruction is quite impossible; when it is possible it produces results of second-class quality as compared with up-to-date field work. To compare such results with modern conditions is hardly ever legitimate. The ethnographer working on the reconstructed past would have to appear before the practical man with, at the best, "damaged goods" in the line of practical advice and theoretical insight. [7] One or two concrete examples may be useful to show the futility of looking to the past for guidance on future policies.

Many African tribes before European contact throve on cannibalism, grew prosperous on slavery or cattle raiding, and developed their political power by intertribal warfare. Would any anthropologist therefore advocate a return to a human flesh diet, or to slavery, warfare, and expeditions for loot and booty? Hardly. But does even the fact that his great-grandfathers were accustomed to gorge themselves on human flesh affect in any way, direct or indirect, the desirable diet of a small child in an urban location; or that of a mine laborer; or a member of a tribe who have to devise a new economy because their territory has been cut down, their pastures eroded, and their taxation increased? These questions supply their own answers.

The economic resources of African tribes have changed: African enterprise has grown in some districts, and in many respects out of all proportion to old conditions; while some of their pursuits have been rendered completely obscure. In political matters the chief can no longer use his armed forces to increase his revenue or to enforce his whims and wishes; he cannot be allowed to use forced labor, still less to indulge in the capture and trade of slaves; his religious power has

6. Both quotations come from p. 1, *Reaction to Conquest,* which in my opinion will always rank not only as a pioneering study of culture change but as a model of modern scientific field work.

7. As we shall see later, it is possible to develop other criteria, and all our writers have either explicitly or implicitly made other suggestions very much more fruitful than that of reconstructing zero point. In their published work, all of them have actually used methods of field work and devices completely satisfactory from every point of view. Dr. Mair's leading article is excellent as an introduction to the series. It indicates the relevant questions; lays down some of the main principles, without dogmatically imposing any specific solutions. Here again it must not be forgotten that Dr. Mair is not only writing round culture contact but in her two books, *An African People in the Twentieth Century* (London, 1934) and *Native Policies in Africa* (London, 1936), has proved that she is well able to work on the subject at first hand. Her monograph on the Baganda is an admirable account of an African community in transition. Her theoretical analysis of Native policies in Africa should be read by every contact anthropologist as a first introduction to the wider European setting of the whole question.

been affected by the new beliefs and undermined by new skepticisms. If we were to take one institution after another; if we were to survey the various aspects—economic, legal, educational or political—we should find everywhere that part at least of the "zero conditions" of the historical past, as it existed before the advent of Europeans, is dead and buried, and as such irrelevant.

I have criticized these theories in some detail, because even the exploring of a blind alley here and there is a contribution to the advancement of science. Let us remember too that the concept of culture change as a "mixture" of elements borrowed from parent cultures is suggested to every ethnographer by the dominant school of today, that of Graebner and Pater Schmidt, and most American anthropologists. Again, the search for zero point is nothing but the obvious course to be taken by every field ethnographer, whose task up till now has been the portraying of cultures as they were in their undisturbed state. The method of studying a contact situation as "an integral whole" is one which naturally would appeal to a functionalist. As long as we do not specifically focus our attention on change as a dynamic process, this approach is legitimate within limits.

Nor was our criticism solely negative. At every step of our argument certain constructive principles have emerged, and these combined have allowed us to formulate briefly a systematic approach to the study of culture contact. Thus, in analyzing the concept of culture change as a mixture to be understood only in terms of parent cultures we arrived at a positive definition of the process of change. We came to regard it as a new reality resulting from the interaction of European impact on indigenous cultures. While we deprecated the treatment of European agencies as an integral part of the new combined community, we were able to lay down the threefold scheme of approach—European intentions, surviving African realities, and processes of contact —thus developing and substantiating our conception of change as a constant interaction.

This approach we shall be able to develop into a useful instrument for the direction of field work and the presentation of evidence. Finally, while rejecting the search for zero point as a means of practical control and theoretical insight into the nature of culture change, we replaced it by other conceptions. We made a distinction between the past, dead and buried, and those elements of the old culture which still retain their vitality and influence present conditions—points which will require more detailed treatment in the following chapters. We recognized that the retrospective vision, however erroneous, is more important than the myth unknown or forgotten by old informants.

While reconstruction of the past is interesting historically and theoretically, practically it contains no hints, since there can be no return to what has been destroyed, what has been forgotten, what can never be fostered by the European administration. But we can turn to the surviving traditions of the present, for this is a rich field for study and source of practical difficulties.

Therefore instead of linking up evidence by the coördinate of time and projecting it under the headings of past, present, and future into an evolutionary or historical sequence, we have to marshal the facts under categories, all of which co-exist in the present, all of which can be studied in empirical field work. In introducing thus, in a somewhat schematic manner, some order into the chaos of change and transformation, into the swinging to and fro of African opinions and movements from progress to tradition, and from tribalism to imitation of Europeans, we found it also essential to deal with organized systems of European activities, and to coördinate these directly with corresponding phenomena of change: with those African institutions which are ousted by European influences or have to coöperate with them, which come into direct conflict with them or else complement them. African chieftainship and the incorporation of Indirect Rule into the European administrative system must obviously be considered side by side. Equally the work of missions has to be set against African ancestor worship and African belief in religion and magic. Alongside these two factors from the two cultures we have to study the phenomena of change and transformation, the school in the Bush, the work of the Native congregation in new African sects, and the newly invented African movements of religion.

Whether we deal with every factor under a threefold approach or whether in some cases we find it profitable to add a flanking column in which we add a reconstruction of zero point, which in some cases might be obtainable with a fair degree of approximation, and which we separate from the columns of corporate change, will depend on the nature of the subject and the data at our disposal. In most cases, however, I would plead that the consideration of tendencies and forward movements, such as the African revolt against European innovations, African nationalism, or the recrudescence of tribalism, is more important than harking back to a vanished set of conditions. The forces which are growing, which are real now and may become important in the future are, from a practical point of view, a dominant factor in the situation.

But science works not only by direct application; it learns also from the development of principles, from the development of clear ideas and the lessons which can be drawn from past blunders, misconceptions, and wrong policies. From this point of view history is as important in its past stages as in its assessment of the future. So that while in the elaboration of practical criteria of guidance I have attempted to warn against too much hope from mere reconstructive activity, I would be the last to underrate the value of historical knowledge. "History repeats itself" in the sense that there are universal laws of cultural process. Since these operate independently of time, space, and circumstances, they can be deciphered from any stage of human development, and it is here, in my opinion, that no aspect or phase of anthropological research can ever fail to be useful in the long run.

Let me briefly state the position as it appears to me.[8] History is the reconstruction of the past, based on written documents, as well as on any collateral evidence, archaeological, linguistic, or geographical, which throws light on bygone events and allows retrospective inferences to be drawn with more or less certainty. It is clear, however, that if the reconstruction is not to be carried out by guesswork, it has to proceed by valid inferences, that is, on the foundation of scientific generalizations. Neither the written chronicles nor yet the monuments of the past, least of all collateral evidence, give us a full picture of past happenings. The historian has to use inference, and this is only possible on the basis of universal laws of cultural or sociological process. Whether, as a historian, you have to build up the character of a personality, or the economic conditions of an epoch, or its legal system, you always have to make a somewhat fragmentary evidence tell its tale by building up the whole from its parts; by making inventories, manorial rolls, legal deeds tell the reality not directly contained in them.

The primary interest of the retrospective process is undoubtedly for most historians the knowledge of the integral fact conjured up from the past. But after the reconstruction of full-blooded, live phenomena has been achieved by the scientific technique of using general laws, historical facts do again lend themselves to generalizations. A comparative study of city politics in ancient Greece and Renaissance Italy; theories of revolutionary governments, of dictatorships, of social stratification, property, and the role of war and conquest in human development, can be and have been legitimately built up from reconstructed historical facts. Thus history, which thrives on sociological and cultural generalizations—for without these it becomes mere guess-

8. The following paragraphs (pp. 33-34) are condensed from Malinowski's "The Present State of Studies in Culture Contact: Some Comments on an American Approach," *Africa*, XII (1939), 41-44. Ed.

work—yields again laws of social or cultural science. To oppose history and science is futile. To neglect either of them makes any humanistic pursuit incomplete.

In what way can an ethnographer use his historical sense and pursue historical ends? As a matter of method he differs from the ordinary historian in that he has no written chronicles at his disposal, except, that is, earlier records of field work which, when they are satisfactory, supply him with genuine historical evidence. But in so far as he wishes to reconstruct history within the wider horizons of centuries or millennia, he depends on comparative material.

From this point of view, I think that so-called functionalism is not, and cannot be, opposed to the historical approach but is indeed its necessary complement. The functional method, if I understand it rightly, is interested primarily in the processes of culture as an explanation of its products. It introduces thus the time element, at first on a smaller scale, but nonetheless in the real historical sense. I myself have advocated the biographical approach in the study of kinship. In my work on language, I have attempted to show that the study of meaning should start with the observations on infant speech and the growth of linguistic expression within the context of culture. In the study of law, I have tried to point out that the consideration of transactions in the long run, as the extensive and enduring balancing of interests, is the only way to understand primitive jurisprudence. The context of time as well as the context of culture essential to the functional approach are, on the one hand, historical concepts; and on the other, they lead to the formulation of general laws of process so necessary to any reconstructive work. Here again, therefore, I do not see that functionalism and historical reconstructions stand in antithesis. There is, however, always the proviso that a genuine history of phenomena must study them in their various phases of progress; [9] and that finally, the utility of historical reconstruction must not be confused with a technique of immediate applications in the search for practical criteria in administrative, economic, and educational control.

The Practical Relevance of Surviving Historical Residues

It might be assumed that in a community where half of the institutions have ceased to function and the other half have not yet started, the functional approach would be quite useless. Thus, what is the relevance, except for antiquarian interests, of chieftainship where this institution has become politically atrophied? Is not, for example,

9. End of citation from "The Present State of Studies in Culture Contact."

the whole attitude toward cattle merely a drag and a nuisance, polygamy simply an anachronism, initiation ceremonies, as in South Africa, a superstition practiced out of sheer force of custom and conservatism? On the other hand, European education seems in many respects to have not yet taken sufficient root to be treated as a real force; European administration to be rather a superimposed force, which has to be obeyed whether it is functionally adapted or not; money economy a system which has been introduced from outside by pressure.

In reality, it is just in these studies of culture change that the concept of function can, from the theoretical point of view, be best understood in some of its characteristics, studied in a way in which good research on a fully integrated culture would give no comparable results. Moreover, from the political point of view, it is just the functional approach which should be the alpha and omega of all field work. For example, chieftainship, even when it is politically obsolete, still stands for the principle of authority, as the Natives themselves aver and practice.[10] To study how the tribal principle still survives, how it affects the relation between children and parents, and even school discipline, is of supreme importance, when we consider that authority, discipline, respect for the older generation and for tradition in general are indispensable, in one form or another, for a stable society.

Again the whole problem of overstocking and the other difficulties connected with cattle economics are associated with the old attitude toward cattle. This attitude is held by the Native Economic Commission as the main villain of the plot. In reality, this attitude is a fact and a force. If we want to change it greatly, we must understand it first and foremost. Is the policy of the administration more intelligent? Considering that overstocking is one of the main evils, why introduce forcible dipping against the Natives' wishes, and thus double the quantity of heads of cattle? [11]

With all this, it will still be necessary to enter more fully into the principles of theory and suitable methods of field work by which the study of a partially transformed, fundamentally resistant culture has to be carried out. Detribalism is a piecemeal process, and at first sight somewhat unaccountable and fitful. Certain elements seem to go very easily without yet seriously affecting fundamental institutions. In many tribes Native dress—or the absence thereof—cannot be seen any longer, and European cotton is taken on with surprising rapidity. In

10. For such evidence among the Pondo see Hunter, *Reaction to Conquest,* pp. 427–430.

11. *Vide* Hunter, *idem,* p. 68, where she states that the *Bunga* is attempting to introduce stud stock but has taken no measures to do away with scrub bulls. There are also signs of serious overstocking and consequent erosion.

some areas indigenous sports and games have been largely superseded by football or cricket; tribes change their religion, or dispense with certain rites and ceremonies of ancestor worship, even where cult and belief still survive substantially. No general rule can easily be laid down with any validity for the whole continent.

There are cultural elements which are not allowed to continue because they are repugnant to the Whites. European administration does not allow cannibalism, intertribal warfare, mutilation as legal punishment or as the chief's pastime. Head hunting, witchcraft, ritual obscenities are generally discountenanced, and the traffic in human beings has been abolished throughout the continent.

Yet it is important to realize that from all such cultural factors a more or less substantial residue still survives. War has left behind a military organization which among such nations or tribes as the Ashanti, Masai, the Ngoni, Zulu, or Swazi, to mention only a few, still forms the backbone of the social order. War survives as one of the most powerful traditional elements in the prestige of certain tribes, their national pride in their relation to their neighbors, and even as a serious handicap in their economic attitudes.[12]

Slavery, apart from some remnants of a domestic form, survives in the discrimination of status and legal differences between descendants of slaves and free men. Dr. Richards tells me that many of the Rhodesian tribes on the mines use some of the old categories surviving from slavery to distinguish between recruited and voluntary labor.

Some of the things prohibited and persecuted disappear, but only from the surface of tribal life. They are practiced in secret and exercise an enormous influence on modern African culture.[13] Typical of these is witchcraft. Neither is ancestor worship completely dead in the Christian section of the community. The psychoanalyst would say that it survives in the "collective unconscious" of the Christianized African. But we need not adopt mystical concepts of European origin to describe African mysticisms. Through continued contact with heathens, and also because the tradition of ancestor worship is still strong and firmly rooted in the structure of the family, every nominally Christian child learns a great deal about the influence which the ancestral ghosts exercise and the cult by which they can be propitiated. Under the stress of emotional crisis the indigenous belief becomes stronger than the alien creed. *

12. Cf. Dr. Margaret Read, "Tradition and Prestige among the Ngoni," *Africa*, Vol. IX, No. 4 (1936).

13. Dr. Hunter in *Reaction to Conquest* gives us innumerable examples of such survivals, partly incorporated into Christian ritual but even to a greater extent influencing the behavior of Christians in unorthodox ways.

The legal conceptions which vest criminal retribution in the clan, and enjoin the rule of vendetta or *lex talionis,* are also apt to outlast any official prohibitions. Sex customs and taboos discouraged by some European influences, notably by Christianity, very often are carried out *sub rosa.* Dr. Hunter gives an amusing example of this in quoting the universal belief of Christian Natives that White missionaries also conform to the custom of *Ukumetsha,* which closely corresponds to the Central European institution *Fensterln.*

Thus from the practical point of view it is the history surviving either in live tradition or in institutional working which is important. It seems almost obvious that only what still lives can be of any relevance to those who have to control a Native society; that only those forces of tradition which influence the sentiments of living men and women and mold their present-day attitudes can matter. When change has been violent and the hopes of a new millennium promised by the higher culture are not fulfilled, the Natives' highly colored and retrospective vision of what has been is of even more vital concern to those in power.

When in a European colony Indirect Rule is established, the real question is: how much of the old Native machinery is still alive and ready for use? The very attempt at using this machinery is due to its presumptive strength, prestige, and efficiency. Rooted in the past, it has the support of Native belief, sentiment, and respect for customary law. The anthropologist's practical brief is to discover how much of the institution still exists and what the traditional sources of political power are. He has also to demonstrate the limits of its adaptability to modern conditions. In the incorporation of African bride-price into a code, the practical question is not what this type of legal contract looked like a few generations ago but whether it is still an effective social force and what are the prospects of its further development and readjustment.

Consider an institution which the European influences are tempted not to preserve but if possible to abolish—the girls' initiation ceremonies, especially when these involve clitoridectomy, objectionable to the susceptibilities of the Europeans and objectively unhygienic and even dangerous. Here once more from the practical point of view it is irrelevant what was practiced a few generations ago. What matters are the practices of today, and the mysterious vitality which the whole institution, including the surgical detail, presents against all missionary and educational attacks. Why is it that excessively progressive Native organizations, like the Kikuyu Central Association, have pinned clitoridectomy to their political masthead and are prepared to fight for it alongside Communistic principles and classical education à la Oxford and Cambridge? The anthropological problem here is first of all: what function the initiation rites still perform in the social and moral regulation of reproductive life; how they influence Native ideas on marriage, parenthood, and sexual conduct; and why the apparently extrinsic detail seems to possess such a great sentimental value.

On this latter point it is quite useful to remember that the average religiously minded Jew or Mohammedan regards an uncircumcised male as an unclean beast. There are also Christian sects on record who, like the Russian Skoptsy, practice terrible mutilations—practices which are deeply embedded in their dogmatic ideology. Again, in the history of civilized Europe many battles were fought, human beings killed or burnt at the stake for or against the rite of total immersion in baptism—an unhygienic and apparently extrinsic ceremony. It is important in the study of so-called savage or barbarous customs of the heathen to maintain the same tolerance and sympathy which we apply in the study of ours and of our forefathers'. The point at issue here, however, is that it is the vitality and present-day working of this institution which really matter, and not the institution at any stage in the past, however brilliantly and completely we might be able to reconstruct it.

Thus in initiation ceremonies, it is their educational and integrative value which is important. Ancestor worship we would have to study in its several sociological foundations—in the organization of the family, parenthood, and descent. Here once more the intelligent missionary will try to appreciate the vitality of the belief and consider, in a really Christian spirit, whether a belief based on the deepest human attachments and connected with the most important institution, that of the family, could not be incorporated rather than destroyed. In dealing with witchcraft, what is significant is the cultural reality of the belief, which we have merely succeeded in driving underground.

Therefore questions of the present function of an institution, its vitality and adaptability and not the shape and trappings of the past, are important for the student of culture change in its theoretical and practical aspects.

In all this we have incidentally implied that it is not only to the rigid adherence to certain features from the past that an African institution can owe its strength. Its new lease of life is often due to the fact that it was able to readjust to new conditions. The chief who adopts Christianity becomes the religious leader of his tribesmen in a new guise, but above all he gains the support of a powerful section of the European community. Chieftainship, recognized by the colonial

administration under Indirect Rule, has acquired a new force uncon-
nected with the tribal past. The tardy admission that bride-price is
compatible with Christian ethics and European legal susceptibilities
has made it flourish again among the Southern Bantu as an important
factor of national integration.

As a matter of fact, the careful reader will have noticed in our
analysis of the conditions of vitality of African institutions that constant reference to European influences was implied in such expressions
as "driven underground," "adapted," or "suppressed." For it is European impact which has forced the Africans to give up certain things,
by direct command, by the introduction of new techniques and new
interests, as well as by new material contrivances.

In all the cases where African institutions are allowed to survive,
or even encouraged to do so, the traditional sources of indigenous
vitality and strength are also there. They constitute the real basis for
the persistence of the custom, legal principle, or type of social organization, though they are not the only factor in the chances of future development. It is the combination of the enormous prestige
which in some areas the chief still retains as rain maker or as wielder
of tribal fertility in land, beast, and man; his role as officiator in the
ancestor cult for the community as a whole—it is the combination of
all this with his new recognition as part of the European administrative
machinery which gives chieftainship under Indirect Rule a firm charter
of permanence and strength. When in another district the chief becomes a Christian, he may lose his old religious sanctions but he still
remains the lawful heir in the long line of rulers; he still stands for the
principle of authority for the Natives.

This brings us once more to the question: can we analyze more
fully the problem why certain elements survive and others disappear;
why at times institutions survive by continuing a clandestine existence
below the surface of European notice, and at others by being raised
into the limelight of full European recognition? [14] It is clear that the

14. In this work the differential study of areas, chosen according to the degree of
detribalization, is of the greatest value. This method, advocated by Dr. Richards in an
article which is probably one of the first systematic attempts to define culture contact
problems, involves the selection of a number of typical villages, all exposed to different
types and degrees of contact influences. *Vide* her "Anthropological Problems in North-
Eastern Rhodesia," *Africa*, Vol. V, No. 2 (1932).

In order to do justice to the heterogeneous picture presented in any one village,
Dr. Richards also elaborated a more precise method of investigation, namely, the
analysis of case histories and the use of a questionnaire for compiling a sociological
census. The questions were put to members of the village in a series of house-to-house
visits, so that the answers furnished documents not merely on isolated individuals but
also on families, kinship groups, and clans. This concrete approach through case study
over a large number of samples is indispensable to the study of contact. For an example

very fact of piecemeal transformation, the fitfulness of disappearances in many cultural phenomena, imposes a new and not easy task on the trained fieldworker. He has to show in his picture of the surviving realities of African culture what factors have gone but are remembered; what institutions have been driven underground; and what elements still survive in new combinations.

Can we, however, go beyond the mere cataloguing of residues and deficiencies in indigenous cultures? Is it possible to account for the easy dropping of certain customs and the bitter tenacity with which others are retained?

of the type of questionnaire employed, see Dr. Richards' "The Village Census in the Study of Culture Contact," p. 55.

In Central America, Dr. Robert Redfield has utilized a similar method of making differential studies of communities undergoing change in the one area. He chose for this purpose a city, town, and village in Yucatan, which were in contact with one another. *Vide* his "Culture Changes in Yucatan," *American Anthropologist*, Vol. XXXVI, n.s. (1934). Ed.

IV

THE FUNCTIONAL THEORY OF CULTURE

A MUCH fuller analysis must replace the vague blanket terms employed to describe the phenomena of partial conservatism, of rapid detribalization, of the selection of some elements, and the difficulties of acculturation in other respects. The solution of these problems can only be found through the functional analysis of Native society on the one hand and the appreciation of European give and take on the other. Stress is often laid on the fitful acceptance by the African of our cultural values; but, as we shall see, it is the piecemeal bestowal of cultural benefits on the part of the Europeans which is of far greater importance. To "a selective conservatism" on the African's part there corresponds a selective giving by the Europeans; a selective taking away of such things as land, natural resources, the contribution of African labor, the political sovereignty of rulers, and the social status and self-determination of any and every African. The Europeans do not dispense the bounties and benefits of their culture with any less discrimination than the African shows in taking what is offered to him. Let us turn to the analysis of the forces of conservatism within the African society.

From the point of view of method and theory of field work, the most important principle lies in the functional conception of culture. This declares that to study details detached from their setting must inevitably stultify theory, field work, and practical handling alike. The detail of clitoridectomy in initiation ceremonies has been taken as the butt of European attacks. This has distorted the value and importance of the institution in the eyes of African and European alike. To regard the introduction of a single implement like the plough in isolation from all that it means in revolutionizing Native agriculture leads, as we have seen, into an impasse of research. The main mistake invariably committed in discussions and even in practical measures of Indirect Rule was to regard the chief as the only item worth considering. "In most parts of Africa, finding the chief has been considered equivalent to establishing indirect rule," so Dr. Richards tells us in her admirable article on "Tribal Government in Transition." [1] Again, the piecemeal

1. *Journal of the Royal African Society*, suppl. to Vol. XXXIV (October, 1935). This indictment does not extend to the extremely well-informed, wise, and anthropologically correct proceeding taken at the establishment of Indirect Rule in Tanganyika Territory. The instructions drafted, if I am correct, by Sir Donald Cameron and Sir Philip Mitchell should be read by anthropologist and administrator alike as a model of applied anthropology.

attack on pregnancy taboos, on occasional sexual excesses, and on certain marriage customs in some tribes by missionaries, who have been unable to relate these rites to the fundamental institutions of family and marriage, has been, in my opinion, the main cause of the failure of Christian endeavor in raising permanently the moral standards of the African in those communities.

The modern anthropologist of the functional school is fully aware that he has to organize his evidence, relate the customs, beliefs, ideas, and practices to the fundamental core round which they are built.[2] To the functionalist, culture, that is, the whole body of implements, the charters of its social groups, human ideas, beliefs, and customs, constitutes a vast apparatus by which man is put in a position the better to cope with the concrete, specific problems which face him in his adaptation to his environment in the course of the satisfaction of his needs. Let me give in brief outline the foundations of the functional theory of culture.

It has to be accepted as an axiom that human beings have to be nourished; that they have to reproduce; that they must be provided with shelter, personal comforts, the elements of cleanliness, and a suitable range of temperature. Anthropological theory must take its stand on biological fact. After all, human beings are an animal species. They have to conform to the elementary conditions which have to be fulfilled so that the race may continue, the individual may survive, and the organism be maintained in its working order. Healthy metabolism can only proceed in an organism which is well nourished; which has a supply of oxygen for breathing, and opportunities for muscular movement and nervous relaxation.

So far so good. But it might be maintained, as is done by some sociologists, for instance Durkheim, that the subject matter of social science and that of physiology have to be kept strictly apart. This is not possible. For although human beings are animals, they are animals who live not by physiological drives alone but by physiological drives molded and modified by the conditions of culture. The food on which the Central Australian or Bushman subsists would not be acceptable to a European. In order to survive on it, his organism would have to be reconditioned by a severe process of secondary training. Propagation does not take place among human beings by simple mating but within the highly complicated cultural institution of marriage. Kin-

2. The following exposition (pp. 42 ff.) of the functional theory of culture is taken from Malinowski's article, "The Scientific Basis of Applied Anthropology," Reale Accademia d'Italia, Fondazione Alessandro Volta, Estratto dagli Atti dell' VIII Convegno (Rome, 1938; published, 1940), XVI, 22. Ed.

ship and sexual attraction are determined under conditions of culture, not by physiological drives alone but by those combined with the desire for companionship, by the need of economic coöperation, by social rank and spiritual compatibility. And this is profoundly determined by the fact that the sexual impulse does not and cannot alone lead to the production of new human beings. The procreative act has its educational, economic, legal, and moral consequences. Bodily movement does not proceed on purely instinctive lines but is organized in a great variety of human species which we call tribes, nations, and cultures, into highly complicated specific activities connected with technology, transport, games, and economic pursuits. It would be possible to show that even such processes as breathing, digestion, sleep, and exposure to sun, wind, and weather are, in the human species, never controlled by innate physiological reflexes alone but are modified by cultural determinants. Human impulses—the tastes which lead man to discriminate, the drives which move man and woman to action—are dictated by a physiology refashioned into acquired habit.

From this point of view, culture appears as a vast conditioning apparatus which, through training, the imparting of skills, the teaching of norms, and the development of tastes, amalgamates nurture with nature, and produces beings whose behavior cannot be determined by the study of anatomy and physiology alone. All this means that man, unlike the animal, never satisfies his bodily needs directly. He obtains his nourishment, not by repairing to a vast larder provided by the environment, but through a more or less round-about process which is the economic exploitation of the environment. Even the simplest food-collecting peoples organize their root digging, their search for small animals and edible fruit; they preserve and distribute this food, prepare and consume it in organized groups. The human body, even among those people who have no clothes to speak of, is not exposed to wind, weather, and sunshine directly. It is protected by a cultural carapace of windshield or house; it is warmed by a fire, screened against wind or sunshine. Again, man never deals with his difficulties alone. He organizes into families; he lives in a community with a tribal constitution, where principles of authority, of leadership, of hierarchy are defined by a cultural charter.

But technical skills as well as organization are based on one more specifically human characteristic: the development of symbolism, that is, of abstract concepts primarily embodied in language. This is, again, a capacity which gives man a special place in animal creation closely associated with the anatomical development of his brain. Language and abstract thought are the vehicles of knowledge, of belief, of legal systems and tribal constitutions. Through the use of language, tradition and education, that is, the continuance of tradition, are made possible. The individual experience of a lifetime is transformed into the collective knowledge of mankind, at times limited, but again, as we see in our own civilization, leading man to an undreamed mastery over the environment.

We have started from the axiom that culture is an instrumental reality, an apparatus for the satisfaction of fundamental needs, that is, organic survival, environmental adaptation, and continuity in the biological sense. To this we have added the empirical corollary that, under conditions of culture, the satisfaction of organic needs is achieved in an indirect, round-about manner. Man uses tools; covers himself with clothes, and shelters himself in caves or huts, windshields or tents. He uses fire for warmth and for cooking. In this, he transforms his anatomical endowments in all his contacts with the physical milieu. He does this not alone but organized into groups. Organization means the tradition of skills, of knowledge, and of values.

Our argument thus leads us to the conclusion that the cultural satisfaction of primary biological needs imposes upon man secondary or derived imperatives. Thus, the whole body of material apparatus must be produced, maintained, distributed, used, and valued. Some economic organization, however rudimentary, is indispensable to every human society. It consists in a system of traditional rules, of technique, of property, and of the way of using and consuming objects. The functional approach to the comparative study of cultures thus postulates that the study of systems of production, distribution, and consumption must be carried out, even in the most primitive societies. It must be primarily directed toward the establishment of such concepts as property, especially property in land, division of labor, incentives, wealth, and value. Value as the main motive of organized human effort, as the principle by which human beings are made to coöperate, to produce, to maintain wealth, and to surround it with religious and sentimental beliefs, must exist even at the most primitive stages of development.

In this, we have defined the economic aspect in the comparative study of cultures. We have laid down the principle that some form or other of economic system is a universal feature of all organized human life, since it corresponds to a universal, albeit derived, imperative.

Another derived, yet universal, aspect of all culture is the one which might be described as normative. Man achieves his mastery over the environment and his competitors through coöperation. Coöperation means life in common. Both coöperation and life in common imply sacrifices and joint effort, subordination of private interests to mutual

were in danger of confusing the teachings of experience and reason with a gust of mystical phantasy. The very fact that some of the most primitive peoples known, the Australian aborigines, produce and have produced generation after generation such a highly complicated implement as the boomerang—the theory of which requires mathematical calculus to explain its construction and flight—shows how carefully and jealously a strictly scientific achievement can be maintained in a primitive culture. Thus knowledge as the capacity to distinguish empirical fact and sound reasoning, and to follow their biddings integrally, is an implication of all cultural behavior even at the most primitive stages.

Knowledge which establishes man's final superiority over the animal world has, however, also imposed on him certain burdens. For knowledge is impossible without the formation of systems, while foresight and constructive thought are of the very essence of science. But the use of knowledge reveals to man the fundamental uncertainty and limitations of his own existence. Man, however primitive, has to think clearly. He has to look back and remember. He must also look ahead and foresee, and readapt his past experience. But although man lives reasonably, even at the early stages of his development, he does not live by reason alone. Memory and foresight, constructive thought and anticipation, refer to matters on which human welfare and the satisfaction of man's needs are intrinsically dependent. Here man's emotional reactions come into play. His very calculations and systematic thought make him subject to fear as well as to hope; to desire as well as to uncertainty. Man of all the animals does not live in the present. Culture makes it impossible for him to lead a hand-to-mouth existence, from moment to moment, in the spiritual as well as in the material sense.

The most reasonable calculations of man have never solved for him practically or emotionally the problems connected with death, with misfortune, with natural catastrophes, such as drought and rain, earthquakes, and outbreaks of pestilence. Let us realize that the occurrence of such acts of destiny do not merely provoke reflection and thought. They force the human group to take action. The death of an individual disorganizes the group. It breaks through the plans in which he might have acted as a leader or adviser. Such an event also shatters every individual personally, in that it forces him to reflect on his own destiny and future.

When we consider the primitive systems of religion and magic, of animism and nature worship, in conjunction with the human psychology of thwarted hope, of fears and anxieties aroused, and of calculations destroyed by an act of destiny, we see that religious belief and ritual contain an organized and standardized response. In the ritual behavior of human groups at burial and mourning, at commemorative ceremonies and sacrifices to the dead, we find first and foremost the affirmation of the belief in human immortality; the conviction that death is not real; that man has a soul, and that this perisheth not—beliefs arising out of the deep need to overcome the fear of personal destruction. This need is not due to any psychological "instinct." It is determined by the cultural factors of coöperation and by the growth of human sentiments in the family, in the comradeship of joint work, and joint responsibility. In all the facts of animism and ancestor worship, of the cult of the dead, and the communion between them and the living, we see a constructive, pragmatically valuable denial of death, and affirmation of the permanence of human values and the reality of human hopes.

Those aspects of religion in which the crises of life are sacralized, that is, made valuable, important, and legally relevant, have again an influence both on social cohesion and on the development of the individual's moral character. The mythology of religion, so intimately bound up with the social structure of a community, with its ritual, and even with its practical concerns, once more has to be considered as something which in virtue of sacred precedent determines the moral, legal, and ritual behavior of the people.

Enough has been said, however, to show that to the functionalist religion is not a cultural epiphenomenon but a profound moral and social force which gives the ultimate integration to human culture. What is usually called magic, and often dismissed as primitive and abortive science, is also a pragmatically important cultural force. A careful study of the contextual influence of magic would reveal first and foremost that magic never encroaches on the technique or subject matter of practical work. Whenever in a culture full technical control has been achieved over certain processes, magic never enters into the manipulation of such processes. Thus, for instance, magic never occurs in fire-making, in the production of stone implements, in the making of pottery, in cooking, in cleaning, or in washing. But in any type of activity where chance and uncontrollable forces are likely to upset human reckoning, magic invariably comes in. Thus in war and courtship, in pursuits dependent on rain and drought, wind and tide, we have inevitably magical beliefs and ritual. A careful and close analysis of the relations between magical acts and practical work reveals moreover that, psychologically, magic leads to the mental integration of the individual, by establishing the positive diathesis of optimism and confidence in success. For magic in its essence is the conviction that, by the utterance of the appropriate spell and the performance of correct ritual gestures, man can bind and bend to his will all that is incalculable, dangerous, and adverse in the potentialities of chance. Magic, in short, is a supernatural technique by which man can, in his conceit, bring about all that which his rational technique fails to accomplish. Wherever magic is carried out on a large scale and on behalf of organized groups of people, magic also establishes leadership, enhances organization, and provides an additional factor in discipline, order, and mutual reliance.

I shall only touch briefly upon that complex, extremely important aspect of culture which concerns the creative activities of man in dancing and decorative art, in the early uses of language for art's sake, and in music. All artistic activities are, on the one side, founded on the physiology of sense-stimulation and muscular as well as nervous processes. The other functional aspect of art, as well as sport, games, and amusements, has a greater practical importance for the anthropologist. For all forms of relaxation and artistic stimulation of the nerves and muscular system are, on the one hand, a condition of healthy communal life, and on the other, fertilizing factors in cultural development and progress.

There is a theoretical aspect on which I have not yet fully insisted, and which can only be briefly indicated. It amounts to the fact that, in the study of every organized human group, it is necessary to document the results by a full inventory of the material apparatus used in its activities; it is essential to see how the group of people itself is constituted and organized; last but not least, linguistic documentation of the crucial concepts, texts, and sayings is indispensable. I would challenge anyone to adduce a single material object which could not be placed in an organized institutional system. No linguistic usage could be found for which a place in a traditional form of coöperation could not be assigned. The study of social organization remains void and suspended in the air unless we correlate it with its concrete place in the environment and lay down its legal charter in terms of Native texts.

In this argument there is thus implied yet another important concept of functional analysis: that of *Institution*, or organized system of human activities. This arises out of the principle just elaborated that the so-called elements or "traits" of a culture do not form a medley of words, implements, ideas, beliefs, customs, myths, and legal principles but are always integrated into well-defined units, for which we

Institutions

have chosen the name institution. We can define an institution as: a group of people united for the pursuit of a simple or complex activity; always in possession of a material endowment and a technical outfit; organized on a definite legal or customary charter, linguistically formulated in myth, legend, rule, and maxim; and trained or prepared for the carrying out of its task.[3]

Family

The importance of this concept consists in that the same institutions occur throughout the whole range of human cultures. The family, that is, the group consisting of husband, wife, and their children, is universal. The tasks for which they are bound—by the charter of legal marriage—are procreation, the joint production and consumption within the household, the education and care of the children, and the carrying out of domestic duties. The charter of the family, moreover, includes the definition of the legitimacy of children, rules of descent, the apportionment of authority in the family, the division of labor, and other economic functions. The family is always associated with a type of habitation; it centers round the domestic hearth, and is endowed with family lands and other possessions.

What has just been said constitutes a universal definition of the family. Every fieldworker may well apply this definition to his particular culture and produce a concrete statement as to whether the family is based on patrilineal or matrilineal marriage; associated with the patrilocal or matrilocal principle; based on a contract validated by an economic transaction, or by an exchange of relatives, or, again, is an undertaking of reciprocal services.

In a similar way it is possible to define the extended kinship group; clan, local, or municipal community; the concept of tribe and that of nation. There exist also typical institutions of less universal occurrence. Thus in some communities we find formalized age grades, again, with their charter of seniority and admission to each class; with various functions—military, economic, ceremonial, and juridical; and with such material equipment as bachelors' and spinsters' houses, ter-

3. In a more recent article, entitled "Man's Culture and Man's Behavior," *Sigma Xi Quarterly*, Vols. XXIX, XXX (1941–42), Malinowski has defined institutions as "groups of people united by common interest, endowed with material equipment, following rules of their tradition or agreement, and contributing towards the work of the culture as a whole." Later in the article he reduces an institution to a diagrammatic form, of which the elements are: charter, personnel, norms, material apparatus, activities and function. He then states: "It can be read as follows: human beings organize under a charter that defines their common aims and that also determines the personnel and the norms of conduct of the group. Applying these norms and with the use of the material apparatus, the members engage in activities, through which they contribute towards the integral function of the institution" (XXX, 74–75). Ed.

ritorial spots for initiation rites, and also economic property owned conjointly by the age group.

If we were to scrutinize the way in which such aspects as economics, political organization, law, or education are worked out concretely, we would find that within each of them there exist professional or occupational groups of people, carrying out a particular type of activity in an organized manner. Thus our aspect of economics describes the general phases of the process: production, exchange, and consumption. In concrete reality we would find, however, that production may consist of agriculture, cattle herding, or industry. Agriculture at times is carried on on the basis of the family, in which case this institution is also the productive agricultural unit. More frequently we find that the tilling of the soil mobilizes a special team of people, under the leadership of the chief, the local headman, or perhaps the man who carries out garden magic. Such a team again is an institution in that it works under the charter of land tenure; of exchange of services; and the apportionment of the crops, including tribute to chief, headman, or magician. The group who jointly till the soil are also the owners of the territory, which may be individually held under joint control. In the administration of justice, we may have, as already elaborated, a more or less crystallized system of guardians and wielders of customary law, or else the knowledge of the rules and their administration may fall within the purview of groups organized on other principles. Disputes about land or produce are usually settled within the agricultural team, the leader and his assistant acting as the impartial authority. Domestic quarrels seldom go beyond the authority of the patriarch or matriarch within the household.

Exactly as the analysis into aspects shows that the types of human activity can be classified into several categories, each comparable with its counterpart in other cultures, and each definable in terms of structure and process, so any attempt at synthesizing, at placing an object, custom, or idea, within its natural setting, brings us to an institution, that is, to an organized, purposeful system of human effort and achievement.[4]

4. For further details on the functional theory of culture the reader is referred to other articles by Malinowski: "Culture," *Encyclopedia of the Social Sciences*, IV (1931); "Anthropology as Basis of Social Science," *Human Affairs* (1937), edited by R. B. Cattell; and "Man's Culture and Man's Behavior," *Sigma Xi Quarterly*, Vols. XXIX, XXX (1941–42). Ed.

V

THE FUNCTION AND ADAPTABILITY OF AFRICAN INSTITUTIONS

ONCE we have grasped the functional approach to culture, we see immediately that while it may seem easy to replace a custom here and there or transform a technical device, such a change of detail very often upsets an institution without reforming it, because, as we have shown, beliefs, ideas, and practices are welded into bigger systems. When we come to the integral institutions of a tribe or a nation, matters become extremely complicated. And the reason for this is that an important institution like the family or chieftainship, ancestor worship or agriculture, has its roots in all aspects of culture. It is connected with so many cultural realities, some of which it is by no means easy to alter, that nothing except a complete transformation of the whole society can provide a painless change, free from maladjustments. Thus the African family, plus polygyny, plus matriliny, plus bride-price, could be replaced by a patriarchal, Christian family based on Roman Law, the Code Napoléon, or English Civil Law. But such a change could only be achieved by transforming the whole society simultaneously, and by giving the necessary wherewithal to establish the new and more elaborate type. One kind of institution can be replaced by another which fulfills a similar function. But such change is difficult, and it always has to move toward something which is better in the cultural sense, that is, better endowed, giving greater scope and opportunities to the people who live in that institution.

Let me, however, give one or two examples. Chieftainship shows such a great strength and endurance because it is associated with the local religion and magical beliefs; with the tribesmen's acceptance of customary law as the only adequate expression of right and wrong. Chieftainship is often based on the Native system of kinship, and it represents the principle of family authority in an extended and glorified form. It is the embodiment of past history, of all that is magnificent in it. In order to uproot chieftainship completely it would be necessary to change law and religion, to refashion family life, and to stamp out all the memories of the past. Not only that, it would be essential to synchronize all these changes, to control them carefully through the transition period; to understand, to plan, to advise, and, as we shall see presently, above all to pay for this in hard cash and its many equivalents.

The real power of ancestor worship lies in its deep association with the constitution of the African family. It survives therefore often in its social and ethical aspects, even when on the surface it has been superseded by Christianity. At times it manifests itself in cases of tribal calamity or individual mishap. And it is often revived as an element in the new separatist Christian movements. Bride-price or *lobola* has shown great tenacity as well as plasticity. It has reappeared under new forms and with a partly changed meaning simply because its real nature was not the purchase of a girl by a man but the establishment of legitimacy, a guarantee for the stability of marriage, and an equitable equivalent for the loss to her parental family of her productive power. Bride-price, through its manifold and far-reaching consequences which endure throughout the whole of married life, therefore exercises a strong legal, moral, and economic influence on marriage and parenthood; on the conduct between husband and wife, parents and children, as well as on descent, succession, and inheritance. The initiation ceremonies of girls have everywhere a certain educational value, and act as a mechanism for the development of domestic qualities. But they display the greatest vitality in those tribes where they are intimately associated with strong principles as to the sexual conduct of girls, as among the Chagga and Kikuyu.

All this refers to the forces of conservatism inherent in Native institutions. A comprehensive institution endures because it is organically connected and satisfies an essential need of society. It can be suppressed, but is then driven underground. It can be mutilated, deprived of this or that aspect or prerogative, but it disappears only with the destruction of the whole cultural identity of a people. Either this, or else it can be replaced by a more adequate institution, fulfilling the same function, satisfying the same needs, and conforming, let us say, to the standards of Western civilization. But the complete extinction of really effective authority, of an orderly way of carrying out the business of procreation, of safeguarding property and maintaining law and order, of producing food and other necessities for society, would result in complete anarchy and disorganization. In fact there are sections of detribalized Africa where something like such a state as this already exists in some respects.[1]

So far we have laid the emphasis on one side of the picture. An attempt was made to show why an indefinitely ramified, dovetailing and intertwined reality of culture, an institution, as we have called it, cannot be easily, in a piecemeal fashion, dropped out of a Native cul-

1. For example in the floating population of the copper belt and in the lowest Black proletariat of Native townships and locations.

ture. There is the other aspect. Just because fundamental institutions in each culture correspond to fundamental needs, just because the most important institutions are universal, it is obvious that culture change is possible. The functional approach proves that under certain conditions it could be made easy were it not for the resistance, inevitable and spurious, which comes remarkably enough more from the European than from the African community. One main difficulty we have already discussed, namely, that while change is possible, in order for it to be satisfactory, permanent, and real, it must be complete, in the sense that an equilibrium is again restored among all the institutions which together constitute the culture. But this is not all.

Although there exists a very far-going correspondence between the institutions of various peoples and cultures, such institutions at the same time are not identical. Like every theory which claims to provide a sound basis for comparative work, our analysis satisfies two fundamental conditions: it gives a common measure of comparison, and it insists on the diversity of the concrete manifestations. In so far as every culture has to solve the same set of fundamental problems, there does exist a universal scheme of human cultures. In so far as each cultural problem can be solved by a range of concrete adaptations, there must be a variety of responses. We thus speak of a specific cultural determinism in each ethnographic area. These two principles are not contradictory but complementary.

Hence in all cultures we find the family, authority, law, religion, art, and recreation. They have the same substance in all climes, with all races, and at all levels of development. At the same time, each institution and each aspect of a concrete individual culture is adapted to the environment, and it certainly depends on the evolutionary stage reached by the people. Round the essential core of each institution there grows in the course of history a specific form to which the people naturally cling, not simply because it is congenial to them racially but because at every point it touches the familiar physical environment, is connected with their mode of settlement, their economic pursuits, and their natural resources.

For example, the African chief is a rain maker, especially in districts where fertility depends on the timely incidence of rain and sunshine. The legends and historical glories of an African monarchy are tangible and real. The local traces of monuments, real and supernatural, can be pointed out with the finger. Not only that, but the African chief is there. He can be seen. His power has been felt for generations, at times as cruel willfullness, at times as a beneficent and protective token of security. His generosity has extended to father and grandfather, and can still be appreciated and enjoyed. Can we really say that in any tribe the local chief or king can be replaced by what to the Natives is really a figment, a faraway sovereign, president, or dictator?

The coronation ceremony at Westminster is not as impressive to those who cannot see, listen in, or even read about it, as an African Enstoolment. The personalities of M. le Brun, King George, and even Mussolini lack contour and reality. In this one example we see that in order effectively to substitute the European "chief" for the African the whole situation would have to be transformed for the African. Now this is not impossible—at a price. You could make the African chief into a European princelet, perhaps even dictator; or you could see to it that the European king is brought home to the African. The second alternative is physically impossible. King George cannot spend even a couple of weeks in every African tribe. It is only with the greatest effort that he could go to the Indian Durbar, though there is really a concrete example of what the present argument means. The first course, that is, to make an African kingship into a European principality, would be possible, if one were prepared to spend all the money necessary in order to establish an equivalent (or caricature) of say a small German prewar principality in Africa. This obviously is not a serious proposition. On the other hand, many pro-Natives, missionaries, and educationalists are hoping and working for the establishment of a Christian and Western family in Africa in lieu of the indigenous form. An impossible task? By no means. It has been achieved sporadically and on a very small scale. But to achieve this throughout the continent it would be necessary to provide every household with an apartment, adequate means of education, and of course an economic basis corresponding to the standard of living of even a poor Christian family in Europe.

What has been said of chieftainship and the family refers to every institution, every calling, or profession. The transition from the relatively simple status of an African to that of a civilized Christian and European citizen requires above all substance. You can be a totemist on a few grubs per annum; the pastoral Masai can live on his small herd of cows. But to be a good Christian, a gentleman, Black or White, well educated, clean, respectable, and responsible, ready to coöperate with any other civilized person, you must have economic security, enjoy full social status and, of course, complete control over your own body (including its labor), and freedom from innumerable police regulations. To be civilized and destitute often means to be revolutionary and unreliable. The "Poor White" is a serious problem wherever he occurs. The "Poor Black" becomes a problem when he has been given that one half of civilization which raises ambition and establishes claims but does nothing to satisfy them.

Thus successful culture change in Africa demands enormous expenditure. For it is one of the soundest and most important principles of social science that people are prepared to pass only from worse to better. Only such change is encompassed without much friction and with relative rapidity. This of course is the reason why the national minorities in the United States changed culturally with comparatively amazing ease, with little resistance, and with a rapidity incredible to a European brought up as one of a minority. The sixteen million Poles in Europe remained true to their culture, that is, nationality, for 150 years of Prussian persecution and superhuman efforts to denationalize them. More than a quarter of that number have already been absorbed painlessly into the American nation. The main reason for this, though there are also others, is that in the United States they are offered all along the line substantial economic, political, and social advantages, which was by no means the case under Russian or Prussian rule.

As regards the possibility of a complete transformation of an African tribe into a Black European community, it would be difficult for the anthropologist to foretell how far this might be achieved without any residual difference. Certainly it would be necessary to equip the new community with all those requirements, mostly material, on which a Western community must be founded; to provide it with a sufficiency of natural resources in land and raw materials, and with capital; and also give it the opportunity not only of receiving but of producing the technical devices which are essential to a Western society. Granted this, we can reproduce a bigger and better Harlem or parts of Jamaica or the Southern States anywhere in Africa.

Do we, however, offer the benefits of our culture all along the line to Africans living in those territories where there is a considerable number of European settlers? It has been argued that culture change when it involves the really important factors, that is, institutions, cannot be successful if it be piecemeal. Hence a cultural give and take, in which the give is extremely selective, presents an entirely different problem from the situation in which the African would only have to take what he likes from our Western civilization. But we do not give any African people under our control the following elements of our culture:

1. We do not give them the instruments of physical power: firearms, bombing planes, poison gas, and all that makes effective defense or aggression possible.

2. We do not give our instruments of political mastery. Sovereignty remains vested in the British or Belgian Crown, French Republic, or Italian or Portuguese dictatorship. The Natives, except for an insignificant minority, have no votes. They are not equal citizens of the empire, republic, or dictatorship. Even when they are given Indirect Rule, this is done under control.

3. We do not, in most territories, share with them the substance of economic wealth and advantages. The metal which comes from the gold or copper mines does not flow into African channels, except the inadequate wage. Even when, under indirect economic exploitation as in West Africa and Uganda, we allow the Natives a share of profits, the full control of economic organization remains in the hands of Western enterprise.

4. We do not usually admit them as equals to church assembly, schools, or drawing room. Under some colonial systems, notably the French, African individuals can climb high in the political hierarchy. In British West Africa, race discrimination is less sharp than in the East or South, but full political, social, and even religious equality is nowhere granted.

In fact, from all the points enumerated here, it would be easy to see that it is not a matter of "give," nor yet a matter of generous "offering," but usually a matter of "take." Lands have been to a large extent alienated, usually in the most fruitful regions, from Africans in the Union, in Basutoland, Swaziland, and Kenya. Tribal sovereignty and the indulgence in warfare, which the African valued even as we seem to value it, have been taken away from him. He is being taxed, but the disposal of the funds thus provided is not always under his control, and never completely so.

There is no doubt that, as against this, another long list could be drafted, including all that Europeans have done for the African in good-will, self-sacrifice, and disinterested purpose. The Europeans have given schools, medical services, and they have also tried to evangelize the Natives. In some ways they have given the African a more effective administration; they have opened up the continent with a set of roads, railways, and airways. The African is to a certain extent allowed to benefit by some of these advantages of a more highly developed civilization. But in assessing the value of the things given as against those taken away, we must not forget that, when it comes to spiritual gifts, it is easy to give but difficult to accept. Material advantages, on the other hand, are easily accepted but only relinquished with reluctance. Yet it is just the spiritual gifts with which we are most generous, while we withhold wealth, power, independence, and social equality. Even when it comes to spiritual gifts, we often hand out the shadow and not the substance. The South African Bantu, for example, is educated only so far as is regarded as convenient for the European community; when he is allowed to proceed further with his schooling, he is often educated to a condition of life which he is not permitted to lead.[2] We also give him advice in the form of our religion. At times this is so puritanic and high-pitched in its ideals as to lead the Native into hypocrisy and to divorce him from the ordinary pleasures of his tribal life. The Christian preaches to him the brotherhood of all men as children of God. But European practice makes him realize that colored Christians are divided from White Christians by the inevitable bar in church and factory, on the recreation ground, or on the streets of Johannesburg or Nairobi.

This argument may be mistaken by the superficial reader as an outburst of pro-Native ranting. It is nothing of the sort. All this is simply a statement of one of the most scientifically relevant factors in culture change as it occurs in parts of Africa. To ignore the fact that there is a selective giving on the part of the Europeans makes for a distortion of evidence, and this is a sin against science. Selective giving influences the process of change perhaps more than any other element in the situation. The selective withholdings on the part of the Europeans is both significant and well determined. It is really the withdrawal from culture contact of all those elements which make up the full benefits—economic, political, and legal—of the higher culture. If power, wealth, and social amenities were given, culture change would be a comparatively easy and smooth process. It is the absence of these factors—our selective giving—which makes culture change such a complicated and difficult process. The real forces for effective assimilation are to be found in the advantages offered by us to the accepting culture. If we educate the Africans by giving them book learning, this above all raises the standard of their expectations, and they learn to appreciate our greater political force, the value of economic wealth, the importance of privilege and social position. If, at the same time that we open before them wider horizons, intellectually and emotionally, we also slam the door to all ensuing advantage, as has often been done in South Africa, this obviously produces disastrous effects,

2. Since this was written a report drawn up by the Subcommittee of the Advisory Committee on Education in the Colonies has been issued (1943) which contains recommendations on mass education in Africa. It insists on a speeding up of educational advancement and on the development of new techniques for educational problems in particular localities. A Commission of Enquiry into Higher Education in West Africa has also been appointed. This movement for reform should be borne in mind in reading the analysis of education in the following chapter. Ed.

both on the individual morale and on the possibilities of cultural adjustment.[3]

We had to abandon the mechanical concept of the mixture of cultural elements. We also see how unreal is the view of Black and White forming a well-integrated whole in a situation in which the color bar cuts right across the very determinism in the process of cultural give. The color bar, wherever it enters into the phases and details of culture change, has to be put on the methodological map, not as a political indictment but as a theoretical appreciation of an important force— perhaps the most important of all.

Indeed, the sooner we speak quite freely and openly about it and also with a complete scientific detachment, the better; for the educated Africans are rapidly becoming aware of, and exaggerating, the situation. The African is becoming an anthropologist who turns our own weapons against us. He is studying European aims, pretenses, and all the real and imaginary acts of injustice. Such an anthropology is no doubt mutilated and misguided, full of counter-prejudices, and charged with bitter hostility. It is often blind in its intransigence and sweeping in its wholesale indictment. But it cannot be ignored by the man of science; and it would be better if the practical man did not treat it as a joke or as an insignificant and minor excrescence. For on the whole it contains a great deal of truth, and it foreshadows the formation of a public opinion, of a national and racial feeling which, sooner or later, will have to be taken into account by the practical contact agents.[4]

The intelligent African is rapidly beginning to see that many of the promises contained in European education, in missionary teaching, and even in the good-will of administrative work, are impossible of realization. He begins to see that in spite of his best intentions, the friendly European is not alone. The bulk of White settlers, the man-

3. "I am speaking here, of course, primarily of conditions in British South and East Africa, including the Union. On the surface, conditions in other parts—Portuguese, Belgian, or French—seem to differ. In French Africa, for instance, a small *élite* is given great privileges not granted by British settlers and authorities. But this really means only that the line has a different place, and a somewhat different character. It becomes in reality two lines: that still dividing the *élite* from the Europeans; and the line between the *élite* and the rank and file." Taken from Malinowski's "Modern Anthropology and European Rule in Africa," Reale Accademia d'Italia, Fondazione Alessandro Volta Estratto dagli Atti dell' VIII Convegno (Rome, 1938; published, 1940), XVIII, 20, n. 1. [Tanganyika and Nigeria, as regions in which the policy of Indirect Rule is in force and where the paramountcy of Native interests has been largely observed in practice, fall within a different category. Ed.]

4. The literature produced by the educated Africans, some of whom frame their views with grave moderation and considerable perspicacity, constitutes a body of evidence on which scientific work by a White anthropologist must sooner or later be undertaken. Miss Margery Perham's *Ten Africans* could be read profitably by anyone wishing to obtain a survey of African opinion. Ed.

agers of European enterprise, and all those who have one type of vested interest or another in Africa, have to look after their own side of the dual mandate. The African realizes that he is being thrown back on his own resources. A new conservatism is being born on the rebound. Many of the educated Africans are turning round and beginning to look upon tribalism, not as an object to be despised but as a symbol of their racial heritage, their nationalistic hopes, and of a future cultural independence.

The fact that sexual morality decreases under education, Christianity, and close contact with European life; that marriage and the family disintegrate; that parental authority as well as respect for law and custom decline—all this is a matter of concern both to sympathetic Europeans and to educated Natives. Forms of the new "African individualism" are one and all negative or pathological phenomena, due partly to the fact that transition means duality of control, and that double morals are hardly ever real morals. Disintegration of the family and kinship solidarity is not due to the influence of the individualism of European culture as against African "communism"; it is a phase which occurs in all societies under the stress of economic misery.

Thus the African in transition finds himself in a no-man's-land, where his old tribal stability, his security as to economic resources, which was safeguarded under the old regime by the solidarity of kinship, have disappeared. The new culture, which has prompted him to give up tribalism, has promised to raise him by education to a standard of life worthy of an educated man. But it has not given him suitable and satisfactory equivalents. It has been unable to give him rights of citizenship regarded as due an educated Westerner; and it has discriminated against him socially on practically every point of the ordinary routine of life.

The old tribalism, as it was before the White man came, is now dead and buried. As such it is irrelevant for culture change and its understanding, and for planning. We see also that the new African millennium, in which the Black man will enjoy the full benefits, spiritual and material, of Western culture, has not yet been realized. It is not likely to be realized for some time to come. But it is the duty of the anthropologist to indicate that while the old tribalism is gone, the new tribalism, as it now survives, is something of the highest value for the happiness of the individual Native and the welfare of the African community; that this new tribalism, if given conditions to develop, carries in it the germs of a future healthy African commonwealth. But if with the best intentions we continue to destroy what has been left of it, we are faced with the birth and growth of new forces of nationalism and racialism, which may be hostile, unmanageable, and dangerous in the long run.[5]

The various movements which have so far appeared have broken down largely because the Natives are not yet ripe for national, well-organized, collective action. By the time, however, when a European power in control may become politically embarrassed and when there is fertile ground for the combination of the Natives from the Lakes to the Cape, such a collective body of opinion may not be an irrelevant factor. The anthropologist should have as one of his duties, not to act as a spy, still less as an *agent provocateur*, but to study the growing forces of Bantu nationalism; to insist as all those with knowledge and foresight do, that an improvement in social and, above all, economic conditions, constitutes the only way out of the difficulty; and that no price is too high to pay to prevent inevitable disaster.

The moral of all this is that the problems in the study of change, of diffusion of culture, of acceptance of our values, laws, and ways are connected with the analysis of the contemporary situation, with the motives, intentions, and ways of action of the European community. The most important problem of culture change can be thus formulated: The Natives are changing and moving towards —? The definition of this blank or X is the all-important element in the problem. Can we guarantee to the Native community and guarantee to ourselves the honesty of our plans: that they, the Africans, will sooner or later be given a major share in the economic resources of their territory, and that they will be educated into taking up a leading part in the management and development of these resources? Can we guarantee that they will be the prospective masters of their own country, and that their religious convictions will secure for them the full dignity of civilized and Christian men which that religion implies? If the answer is in the affirmative, then and then only can we honestly force on them our civilization from its technical side and with its legal, political, and religious contentions. But if not, then it is wiser to allow them a great latitude in self-determination along their historically established cultural lines.[6]

5. I have already discussed such possibilities in an earlier article, "Race and Labour," *The Listener*, Suppl. No. 8 (1930). *Vide* also Hunter, *Reaction to Conquest*, pp. 554 ff. for similar movements among the Pondo.

6. It should be noted here that this analysis applies mainly to conditions in the Union. While legislation for Natives has assumed a more restrictive character in recent years owing to the policy of segregation, there has been at the same time a widespread realization that standards of health, education, agriculture, and living conditions in Native areas must be steadily improved and that ample lands must be provided for economic development. *Vide* Lord Hailey, *An African Survey*, p. 371.

In the same book Lord Hailey suggested the provision of a grant for research in the

Turning once more to the theoretical basis for this discussion of the practical problems of culture contact, we can conclude that:

1. The functional method is adequate because it does not exclude the historical or retrospective points of view. But it also places the *terminus ad quem,* the considerations of the future in its aims, policies, and probable outcome, on the map. It introduces history alive, that is, the survival of the past in myth, in retrospective sentiment, and in institutions *extant.* Change, however revolutionary, does not exterminate the past completely; it transforms it partially or obliterates it under surface phenomena. The fundamental institutions of culture persist, though the form in which they fulfill certain functions may be transformed under the impact of European contact.

2. The functional method urges an integral study, that is, a study of new elements in so far as they have taken root, and in exactly the form in which they have done it. Since, however, the principles of integration are not simple but, through the very fact of change, fall asunder under three main headings, the *Problemstellung* must not be falsely simplified.

Each subject of culture change falls into a tripartite division:

a. European interests.

b. The process of contact, mixture, grafting, and transformation.

c. The reservoir of Native culture—its active, conservative influence.

3. The functional method yields us criteria of maladjustment, not from a moral, sentimental, or arbitrarily normative view, but instrumentally. A functional analysis reveals that culture is a vast apparatus for the satisfaction of needs. Each institution, integrated on a certain principle, has a certain system of needs to satisfy: the family, not merely reproduction and sex, but also education, citizenship, and the foundations of social cohesion; economics—a healthy supply of nutritive values, but also a certain autonomy in all the fundamental needs of a tribal culture. Economic life must be referred to environmental sufficiencies and to a number of social and moral values. The drafting

social and physical sciences, and the establishment of an African Bureau as a clearing house for information (p. 1662). Since that date (1938) a considerable amount of research has been carried out on land tenure, utilization of local resources for economic development, on nutrition, and the effects of European law on Native marriage in Uganda. Early in 1940 a most important decision was made by the British Government to allocate £5 million a year for ten years for colonial development and welfare, and also a further £500,000 a year for research. A Colonial Research Committee was appointed to advise on the organization of research, to deal with specific applications for funds, and to initiate new schemes. For a survey of research carried out in Africa over the last few years, the reader is also referred to "Colonial Research in the British Empire," *Agenda* (October–December, 1942). Ed.

of the African into world economics in a special role as cheap laborer, with all that it implies in mulcting his autonomous economics, is one of the big problems of culture change. In other words, in introducing cultural benefits, even education, European goods, and facilities, the European not only gives but also takes away; and the comparison of how far the gift completely replaces the process subtracted is a constant normative problem of culture change, in which all the elements can yet be scientifically determined.

In all this, the functionalist would obviously suggest, and has *de facto* suggested, the consideration one after another of certain fundamental activities of culture in satisfying certain biological and social needs. The difficulty of cultural transformation, so clearly written all over Africa, is due to two things: first of all, to the complexity and wide ramifications of all organized systems, that is, institutions. Secondly, to the fact that institutions which have grown up in a long historical evolution *in situ* show adaptations to environment, to certain specific local needs, and to the level of culture, and cannot be replaced either piecemeal or in a haphazard way. In short, as we have tried to demonstrate, conservatism or "selective conservatism" is not a sort of mulish obstinacy. It is not due to racial deficiencies. It is an inevitable result of the natural laws of cultural process. Our demonstration does not in any way imply that a transformation is impossible. On the contrary, change though difficult is practicable. But in order to be effective and to produce stability, it will have first of all to be well financed, in the literal sense of the word; and secondly, extremely well engineered, that is, planned on the basis of a sound knowledge of both the aims of transformation (the starting point) and the technical implications.

VI

THE PRINCIPLE OF THE COMMON FACTOR IN CULTURE CHANGE

It is possible now to frame the positive and constructive results emerging from our critical discussions and our survey of evidence.

The African world of contact and change consists of three distinct orders of cultural reality: the African, the Western, and that of transition. Each of these orders is subject to a specific determinism of its own which will be elaborated presently. At the same time, all three orders or phases are related to or dependent on each other. The impact and initiative come from the organized forces of Western civilization. They are directed onto the largely passive tribal resources which respond to contact with adaptation or conflict. This process of reaction, positive or negative—the interaction between Black and White, between Western culture and tribalism—covers the field of contact and change. Between the two boundaries of color bar on the one side and the dead weight of tribal conservatism on the other there lies the no-man's-land of change. This is not a narrow strip but really embraces most of what is going on in Africa. As yet it is but partly accomplished; adaptation is imperfect and piecemeal; conflict is open or concealed; and at times also there is fruitful coöperation or else disorganization and decay.

In this wide area, which is our specific subject of study, European interests and intentions do not act as a united influence. They are largely at war with each other: the genuine tendency to raise the African, and the tendency to keep him back; the gospel of brotherhood and that of the color bar; the discriminative give and the invidious take. The Europeans contribute the initiative and driving force, capital, organization, and technique. They largely determine the form of the new cultural realities, and to a certain extent they still control the process of change. In all this they have to coöperate with and work upon the indigenous humanity who have their own racial characteristics; their institutions of age-long historical growth; their customs, ideas, and beliefs. Once change is set going, it acquires a momentum of its own; becomes a process and a reality *sui generis*, and possesses a cultural determinism which is neither African nor European.

Change cannot be studied by either of the two determinants, African or European, or yet by any device of combining the two. The phenomenon of change is not a mixture; nor even simple acculturation. Change under conditions of the color bar, that is, under conditions where the Black section of the community is not completely, whole-heartedly accepted but on the contrary kept at arm's length—such change becomes a cultural *tertium quid*. Typical facts of change such as Indirect Rule, mining and plantation enterprise, schooling, and so on, obey laws which cannot be deduced from either culture or from both. The working of such contact phenomena, of the coöperation, the conflict, and the reaction, has to be studied in its own right.

Another theoretical by-product of our discussions is that all socio-logically relevant impact and interaction is organized, that is, it occurs as between institutions. The real agencies of contact are organized bodies of human beings working for a definite purpose; handling ap-propriate apparatus of material culture; and subject to a charter of laws, rules, and principles. The chartered company of early days, the European colonial government, the missionary body or the industrial enterprise, a community of planters or settlers—these have been and are the effective influences of the Western world, and each has to direct its impact primarily upon its indigenous counterpart: chief-tainship, African religion, African systems of agriculture, hunting, fishing, or industry. The missionary has to supplant the Native forms of belief and worship, to supplement them or to develop an organized system of African dogma and ritual. The entrepreneur or settler has to appropriate a portion of the natural resources of Africa, exploit them by means of European capital, and use African labor in conjunc-tion with Western techniques and methods of working. In Indirect Rule, European administration with its established force and treasury, with its European-bred tradition of Civil Service, with its bases in the European home country, has to coöperate with an equally strongly welded and traditionally founded Native chieftainship.

Whenever effective coöperation occurs, a new form of social or-ganization is engendered: a Native Christian congregation under the supervision and guidance of a White clergy; a mine or a factory where African labor works under the direction of a White staff; a bush school where African children are taught by European teachers; an organized system of Native administration under European control. Thus what results from impact is not a higgledy-piggledy assortment of traits, but new institutions, organized on a definite charter, run by a mixed per-sonnel, related to European plans, ideas, and needs, and at times satis-fying certain African interests. We find, therefore, that to marshal evidence in any other form than by stating the interaction of two institutions, and the resulting creation of a third composite one, leads theoretically to confusion, and practically to blundering.

The real problems of compatibility, adaptability, and conflict center around the main function and the subsidiary influences of an institution and its constituent factors. And here we come to the concept of the *Common Measure* or the *Common Factor* of interests and intentions. Indeed, this concept seems to me to furnish the clue to all the discussions of change and contact.[1]

The common factor exists wherever there is a long-run identity of interests between Europeans and Africans, as well as competence and knowledge on the part of the Whites in carrying out a well-planned policy. Under such conditions there will be a basis for collaboration and agreement in ideas, sentiments, and general outlook between the two races. Policies of Indirect Rule, of indigenous economic development, of the incorporation of certain African rites into Christian worship, of gradual education with full opportunities for educated Africans, are examples to be found in many parts of the continent, where the existence of the common factor of good-will and converging interests has led to a harmonious process of development. Any analysis of culture change must therefore collate the European intentions or policy with the corresponding African institutions, and assess whether in the process of change the interests of the two sides clash or dovetail.

Difficulties arising out of African land shortage, including overstocking and erosion, the handling of the labor problem, the color-bar principle, are cases of what might be called the "negative common factor," to introduce an arithmetical figment. To destroy something in African life simply because it displeases the Europeans is a classic case of an absence of any common factor, a deficiency which must lead to conflict. Again the African sense of order and respect for law is not fostered but thwarted when the Whites impose burdensome regulations such as pass laws, restrictions on freedom of movement, or deprivation of ordinary privileges in transport, public parks, and other places of amenity. Or to take another example: let us imagine contingents of Natives transported from the reserves into urban locations or made to "squat" on farms, where they have to live under a strictly monetary economy, depending on a wage system. If a study of their budgets shows that their necessary expenditure exceeds their regular

1. The following discussion of the *Common Factor* incorporates material from a lecture given by Malinowski on "Culture Change in Theory and Practice," to the Oxford University Summer School on Colonial Administration, July 5, 1938. Ed.

wages, this is a definite state of maladjustment, an objective symptom of a negative common factor.[2]

The treatment of witchcraft, where the ultimate aim, viz., the abolition of its menace is identical, but the legal methods are based on European ignorance of African mentality and institutions, is another instance of how the common factor in ultimate ends may be vitiated by the absence of the common factor in methods. In the educational system we have another mixed and complicated problem. In so far as the acquisition of European knowledge is advantageous, education has been one of the great forces of uplift. But education may be given merely to make the African a better subject for evangelization; it may be concerned too much with theoretical knowledge, which on the one hand he cannot use to any practical purpose and which on the other hand kindles in him ambitions and just claims, never to be satisfied owing to the European policy of segregation. It may develop technical skills which he will never be able to utilize because of the color-bar discrimination, legal or customary. The educated African convert is then individually and collectively made to suffer for the fact that, owing to his religion and education, he is the equal of his White neighbor. But owing to the color of his skin, he is deprived of political rights, economic opportunities, and the social privileges of equality. Since education is one of the crucial processes in culture change, let us consider it in greater detail from the functional point of view.[3]

Education is a process which starts at birth; it is the social and cultural heritage of the individual. An African is born to a definite tribal status; whether this be of a chief, magician, commoner, warrior, or medicine man matters not. Now, in order to occupy that final position, he has to pass through a Native training.

If you give him a European education, you deprive him of the possibility of a Native training. Here the very common measure of the two determines that you cannot achieve the one without destroying the other. Yet the compatibility and interchangeability of the two phases are demonstrated by the facts. You *can* train Natives to be parsons, teachers, lawyers, and journalists; engineers, skilled workers, and farmers of the European type. Yet the full training of that type re-

2. See the following articles for a detailed discussion of such conditions in rural and urban areas: Ellen Hellman, "Native Life in a Johannesburg Slum," *Africa* (1935); F. W. Fox, "Nutritional Problems amongst the Rural Bantu," *Race Relations*, Vol. VI, No. 1; Hellman, "The Diet of Africans in Johannesburg," *Race Relations*, Vol. VI, No. 1; see also Hunter, *Reaction to Conquest*, pp. 140–141, 450–454, and 516–517, for some specimen budgets and discussion of earnings.

3. See "Native Education and Culture Contact," *International Review of Missions*, Vol. XXV (October, 1936), for a more detailed exposition of Malinowski's views on education. Ed.

quires, above all, opportunities. And here the real difficulty comes in. Full opportunities for professional men, skilled artisans, and workmen, to say nothing of statesmen, financiers, businessmen, require as wide a background of civilization as we have in Europe, and this does not exist in Africa. Nor can it be conjured up as rapidly as the educational processes can produce the unadapted individuals or groups.

Again, the lower ranks of the educational system, which are molded on European patterns, are slavishly given a type of instruction which is useful as a foundation for higher training but mostly a waste of time for an African who needs a minimum of skills and abilities, taught from a very special point of view, if he is to qualify for a position as a servant, an unskilled laborer, a lower government official, or as a member of the police force.

The Europeans, instead of regarding all education or any education as an asset, might consider here that what the African takes from the European culture may be a handicap and a malediction, a blight or an injury, if it opens horizons, develops ambitions, raises him up to a standard of living which cannot be achieved.

The common measure of interest would first of all require a careful consideration of what role the skilled African and the educated African will have to play; what European types of book learning, skill, and ability he will need within the limitations imposed on him by segregation, differential policy, professional disabilities. The principle of common measure declares that only what is effectively useful, both to him and to the European community, should be administered to him educationally, and that in a form directly compatible with his future functions. That such an education should never completely destroy his tribal bonds; estrange him from family and clan; above all, should not make him despise things African, is implied in all the arguments.[4]

Let us glance at the contact problems involved in missionary work. The missionary is the master educator; the master builder of the new African morality; the leader in the appreciation by the African of all that is finest in Western culture. He is often the first to come, and quite as often the last to abandon the ideal attitude in the treatment of African problems. But the missionary is also handicapped by insidious difficulties, incongruities inherent in his work, and obstructive associations. To start with the last named: he has to preach the Gospel of Universal Brotherhood in an atmosphere where this gospel is not always practiced. Indeed, whenever and wherever the principle of the

4. See p. 58, n. 2, where there is a reference to the committees which have been appointed recently (1943) to study these problems. Ed.

color bar is officially (or unofficially) the law of the land, the whole work of the mission is doubly hampered. This negative common factor is expressed in the conflict and incompatibility within the European camp.

Ancestor worship seems to me in many ways the crucial problem and the touchstone of missionary work. It is with regard to this aspect of African culture that the repressive tendency of the mission has hindered the process of evangelization. One of the wrong attitudes to adopt toward ancestor worship is to regard it as entirely reprehensible, simply because it is the core of African paganism and because it involves sacrifice, divination, and communion with ancestors, which seem essentially un-Christian. This is the position which has usually been taken. But a fuller knowledge of ancestor worship in Africa and of religious principles would dictate a different course, one not too late to be adopted in some parts at least. For the principle of ancestor worship itself is as sound a theoretical principle as the Fourth Commandment. To work it gradually into a subordinate position, to make it an outcome of monotheism—in short, to harmonize it completely with the Christian attitude of filial piety and reverence to ancestors—would achieve the same end in a slow and much more effective way. In such a compromise may be found the common factor between Christianity and ancestor worship.

As it is, ancestor worship driven underground survives often in forms of fear and dread, reverted to even by ministers of the Christian religion and always there as a stepping stone to religious separation. In general, the principle of an open and honest expression of mental attitudes is preferable to their violent puritanical suppression. But the most important point about ancestor worship is the fact that it is connected with a type of social organization—the family and the clan; the whole legal system is intimately bound up with it. The complete destruction of the dogma is thus sociologically deleterious. The relegation of the dogma to its proper place, while retaining its social, economic, and legal influences, would produce the same dogmatic results and satisfy the puritanism of the missionary without producing the nefarious results.[5]

5. One of the greatest difficulties in missionary work is sex. An objective and scientific definition of sex morals must be sought, i.e., the type of conduct within the context of a given culture which is in harmony with the institutions of marriage and the family found there. If prenuptial intercourse is allowed as a form of trial marriage, then to abolish it without changing the context is dangerous. It may lead to developments of unnatural vice, of clandestine instead of open fornication. Here it is clear again that parts of an institution ought to be transformed gradually and in harmony with one another.

To sum up the preceding arguments and examples, we can say that wherever there is a common measure between the intentions of European impact and the existing needs of the African society, change can lead to new thriving forms of cultural coöperation. When on the contrary it is, or seems, necessary for the Europeans to take away from the African his territory; to curtail his opportunities; to use his labor to the detriment of Native enterprise without satisfactory remuneration, then the absence of a common factor leads to conflict.

The concept of common measure or common factor is the direct corollary of our principle that human institutions are commensurable across the dividing line of culture; but that in each of these they fulfill the same function under a different type of determinism. The African family and type of marriage are equivalents of European marriage and family. But the legal conception, the safeguards, the type of kinship, differ substantially. In Africa, as in Europe, central authority, education, economic wealth, and value do exist. Each fulfills the same function, and therefore it is possible to implant gradually and constructively European administration, money economy, or book learning in Africa. At the same time, we know that an institution has its legal and religious charter; that it must dispose of a material apparatus; and that it organizes a group of people, united to perform a definite task. Now, if the same group of people has to be reorganized into satisfying some definite need by entirely different means, the process is by no means simple or easy.

Imagine an African agricultural community, and look at them as a food-producing team, that is, an economic institution. There is no reason whatever why we should not in future envisage them as tilling the soil by highly developed methods, using all the modern appliances, with enormously increased output. But in order to achieve this transformation, first and foremost an enormous capital outlay would be necessary; secondly, the legal relation of man to environment would have to be profoundly changed: not only the improvement in land but also new systems of land tenure would have to be introduced. Thirdly, if a surplus of cash crops is produced, opportunities for marketing would have to be created or safeguarded.[6]

There is one more factor which must not be forgotten. The transformation from African tribal agriculture to a highly Western system

6. While nothing on this large scale may be said to have occurred in African communities, it should be noted that commercial crops for export have been grown in certain areas—thus cotton in Uganda, coffee in Tanganyika, and cacao on the West Coast. In view of the points made above, it is significant that on the West Coast the new system of agriculture has resulted in new conceptions of land tenure. *Vide* Lord Hailey, *An African Survey*, p. 884. Ed.

cannot take place overnight. The introduction of the new methods disorganizes the old ones. In order to progress, the African often has to pass through a stage of chaos and disorientation, and he would have to be tided over this stage. In the past such help has usually not been forthcoming. Exactly the same analysis could be made in the matter of administrative change; transition in the organization of family and household; and even more cogently in matters of education, morals, and religion.

The ultimate reality in culture change thus hinges on the fact that corresponding institutions in two cultures satisfy analogous needs in different ways and with different techniques; but in the process they have to use the same human and natural resources: land, capital, labor, politically organized force, the impulses of human reproduction, and also the standardized emotions, values, and loyalties specific to each culture. This means that institutions cannot be replaced rapidly, piecemeal, and without considerable sacrifice on the part of the community which has engendered the change and is carrying it on. On either side of the bar we have the same demand for the limited material resources and limited human energies. It is impossible either to develop the African on his own lines or to change him into a colored Westerner, without leaving him a substantial margin of material prosperity, of political autonomy, and of civic rights. Full development in an economic and spiritual way is also difficult, even perhaps impossible, while we make him feel constantly inferior as regards his racial position and his cultural heritage. Even the maximum of autonomy, economic opportunities, and civic freedom granted to the African would still imply a considerable amount of European control. But all this need not blind us to the fact that if we are to lead the African in the common enterprise of a satisfactory and harmonious transformation; if the African is to coöperate with the European under the terms of the Dual Mandate in exploiting the continent for the world, it is not enough if we supply the spiritual substance and expect the African to give the Marxian quota.

It is in this clash of interests and greeds, as well as in the intrinsic difficulty of piecemeal and institutional change, that the real dynamic issues of contact and change reside. Here, as elsewhere, the only way out of such a difficulty, out of this conflict between the two sets of vested interests, to a certain extent irreconcilable, lies in a compromise. Scientific analysis teaches that the compromise must be real as well as intelligently engineered. The knowledge of facts and an adequately informed framing of policies are indispensable; but let us remember that cold scientific analysis teaches also that the stronger partner cannot rely only on his own intelligence and on feeding the weaker one with fine phrases and good intentions. He must also honestly, albeit with a heavy heart, give up some of his material advantages, some of his privileges, and learn how to share his political influence with the indigenous population. For you cannot develop a strong and healthy culture on anything else but the material basis necessary for it. Nor can you establish a politically sound community if you degrade some of its members into the semblance, at times even the substance, of slaves. Nor yet can you inculcate moral responsibility if you make them feel that no moral justice is exercised toward them.

But although it is the legitimate task of science clearly and forcibly to point out truths, even if these happen to be moral truths, its main business lies on the intellectual side. We have found that the crucial concept of our analysis is that of the common measure. By this we mean the existence of certain elements of common interest, of tasks in which Africans and Europeans can coöperate in their joint interest. The absence of a common factor, or the common factor in its negative form, appears whenever the European in pursuing his own aims has to take away some elements essential to the African's progress; whether this element be land or labor, self-confidence or his own personal dignity; a cherished belief or a type of customary law indispensable to the sound working of marriage, family, or tribal life.

Since this central concept obviously can be defined only as a result of the direct correlation of European and African interests and institutions, the best way of obtaining it is by collating the two cultural realities. Here, as in every scientific work, it is profitable to develop a tangible formal instrument for the handling of evidence. We have already tentatively outlined such a device when discussing the concepts of "mechanical mixture of cultural elements" and "the zero point of tribal culture." We shall see that it will at the same time be useful as a chart for field work, as a method of presenting evidence theoretically, and as a simple and concise way of bringing out practical conclusions.

VII

SCIENTIFIC PRINCIPLES AND INSTRUMENTS IN THE STUDY OF CULTURE CHANGE

THE device here advocated is the translation of the several principles just laid down into a concise diagram. We have found that the two cultural orders, African and European, in their original state entirely independent, and still largely retaining their cultural determinism, meet, impinge on each other, and produce a third cultural reality. Diagrammatically, we shall remain true to this principle in projecting every one of our arguments into three columns. In the first one, Column A, as we can label it throughout, we shall list White influences, interests, and intentions. We shall register there the principles of White policy; the ideals of missionaries; the ends of enterprise; the slogans and real intentions of settlers with regard to any concrete problem, such as land, labor, witchcraft, nutrition, or industry. In Column B, which will be entitled, "Processes of Culture Contact and Change," [1] we shall enter those processes and activities in which Black and White meet, coöperate, and influence each other directly. In Column C we

SPECIMEN CHART TO BE USED FOR THE ANALYSIS OF CULTURE CONTACT AND CHANGE

A	B	C	D	E
WHITE INFLUENCES, INTERESTS, AND INTENTIONS	PROCESSES OF CULTURE CONTACT AND CHANGE	SURVIVING FORMS OF TRADITION	RECONSTRUCTED PAST	NEW FORCES OF SPONTANEOUS AFRICAN REINTEGRATION OR REACTION

shall place the surviving forms of traditional institutions and the memories and legends of past times, in so far as they are active forces in present-day life. This column differs from the preceding one in that it contains elements of African life not recognized officially by the White administration, and processes where the old African life goes on, very often "driven underground" by strong external pressure and internal resistances. For example, we should put here the beliefs,

1. In some of his manuscripts Malinowski has sometimes labeled this column, "Phenomena of Contact and Change." I have selected the above usage as the more dynamic. Ed.

TABLE I

PRINCIPLES

1. The Principle of Autonomous Determinism in each of the three phases:
   A. European intentions and interests,
   B. Contact and change,
   C. Surviving substance of African tribalism.

2. The Principle of Relatedness and Interdependence of the three phases.

3. The Dynamic Asymmetry of European and African cultures respectively in impact and change.

4. Multiplicity and Divergence of European policies, ideas, aims, and methods.

5. Impact and Interaction takes place as between Institutions, i.e., systems of clearly defined activities, carried on by organized groups, associated with some material apparatus, and aiming at the satisfaction of a biological, social, or spiritual need (related activities welded into a permanent system by a charter of laws and customs).

6. Concept of Common Factor—or its absence—between European tendencies and Native interests, as dominating and fundamentally determining the phenomena of change. On the presence or absence of the common factor depends whether there occurs conflict or coöperation (compromise); disintegration or agreement and joint development.

7. Principle of the Vitality of African tribalism resulting from: intrinsic strength of the indigenous culture grown up *in situ;* the selectiveness of European giving; and the effects of a color bar which pushes the African away from any place of vantage in Western civilization, and thrusts him back on to his own tribal resources.

8. The New Nationalism: tribal, regional, African.

TABLE II
RULES OF METHOD

1. Each problem to be studied through the threefold approach. In the diagram we list the European intentions; the phenomena of change; and the facts of African tribalism, each in a separate vertical column.

2. The evidence thus studied and presented under three headings must be related by placing every item in each column against the corresponding evidence in the others. This diagrammatic treatment expresses the correlation of the evidence, European, African, and that of change, bearing upon any given problem.

3. The columns to be placed always in a definite order. European evidence first; African data last; and the facts of change in between, since the last named are the result of the interaction between the two flanking columns. In field work and argument this order expresses the dynamic relation of three phases. Actually, observation and theory may start from any one of the three cultural phases.

4. In Column A we list the various approaches from each European agency or organized body (administrative; missionary; entrepreneur; or settler). We relate to these the corresponding factors in African tribalism; and in the column of change study their interaction.

5. In tabulating, we have to list the charter of an institution; the principles of policy; or the fundamental belief of the religious or magical movement, first. We then consider in turn its sociological aspect; its economic and technical implications. In stating the charter or policy of a European or native institution or movement, it will be necessary to take into account the real cultural function and not merely the catch words or traditional phrasing.

6. The definition of the Common Factor automatically results from the collation of each entry in Columns A and C. The placing of all evidence on change in the central column corresponds to the central importance of the concept of Common Factor. The Common Factor in the first entries, referring to the main function of a policy or movement, defines the prospects of coöperation as against conflict.

7. This contains the definition of what legitimately has to be listed under C; indigenous institutions ignored or suppressed by the Europeans; institutions, beliefs, and practices driven underground; African customs, economic arrangements, and legal principles carried on among detribalized natives. N.B. Column C emphatically must not contain any data obtained by "reconstruction" of the past.

8. The facts of Nationalistic Reaction will have, for purposes of convenience and manageability, to be also listed in Column C.

practices, and ethical influences of ancestor worship such as are actually found even in Christian communities. In discussing land tenure and economic activities, we should have to enter here remnants of old customary law, completely ignored by the European law and the administrative machine, or even at times running counter to influences from Column A.

In order to make our argument clear, it would be useful to attach an additional column, D, containing the reconstruction of the pre-European conditions so far as it is possible to achieve this scientifically by checking. Since this is an essential task of the anthropologist, Column D is a legitimate part of our synoptic scheme, but it is important to realize that it can never be the result of actual observation, and that the validity of the data there presented is of an entirely different order from that of the other three columns. For in A, B, and C, the field-worker gives descriptions of facts actually observed. In Column D he can only state his opinion as to what most probably did exist in a former epoch.

Finally, in some cases it will be relevant to add one more entry. We might register under Column E the new forces of spontaneous African reintegration or reaction. Here would come such phenomena as African racialism, regional nationalism, and the reinterpretation of tribal patriotism. Such facts, as we have already insisted, must be considered by the anthropologist. It is well to separate them from phenomena of coöperative change and culture contact listed in Column B as well as from the archaic elements in Column C.[2]

Since we are devising a method of analysis, as well as of observation and practical argument, which is based on a set of principles and can be represented in a chart (see page 73), it might be best to proceed in the following manner. In the appended tables (pp. 74–75), there are stated on the left side in Table I the principles which we have elaborated in the course of our preceding discussions. Corresponding to each of them there will be found in Table II a definite practical rule, which obviously is at the same time a rule of method in field work, a directing principle in guiding any discussion, and a manner of handling any evidence by the practical man. As with all sound rules of method, those of our right-hand side (Table II) are translatable directly into a chart.

2. Malinowski, in some notes made at Yale University, suggested a further refinement of this chart, namely, the addition of a column to outflank A, where a distinction can be made between Western intentions as being pressed in Europe on the one hand, and Western policy as modified by Europeans in Africa on the other. Ed.

Comment on Table I: Principles

The meaning of the principles should now be quite clear, but one or two concepts which occur in the new wording may still be briefly defined, and in such definition we shall sum up and recrystallize the gist of previous discussions.

Thus in our first principle we have summed up the necessity of the threefold approach and emphasized the fact that each of the three main phases of African cultural reality possesses an autonomous cultural determinism. What is meant by this last phrase should by now be evident. In our critical discussion and rejection of the concept of culture change as an integral whole, and also in elaborating the argument that European giving is as important as African taking, we were constantly faced by the existence of a specific cultural determinism. This means that there are factors and forces which compel man, individually and collectively, to behave in a way specific to each given culture in matters which transcend and modify mere biological impulses and the direct influence of environmental conditions. Each culture develops in the course of its historical evolution systems of knowledge, values—economic, social and aesthetic—and last but not least, beliefs and convictions based on supernatural revelation. Each cultural value or imperative determines conduct in matters as elementary as the preferences for certain types of food and drink; in the responses to the drive of sex and the desire for family life; in the sense of honor, and of right and wrong; in the type and range of amusements; and in objects regarded as culturally valuable. The ends of physical effort and of social competition differ profoundly as between a community of headhunters and cannibals, a totalitarian state, a European nationalistic power, a democracy, or an African monarchy. Even in our own recent history in Europe, we regarded slavery and serfdom as natural institutions and part of the Divine Order of the Universe; we burnt witches; we killed Mohammedans in Crusades; and conducted bloody wars on account of religious ideals. This we have discarded as so much barbarianism or savagery.

It is important to realize that just now in the African world of change and contact there exist three main types of cultural determinism. The members of the Western civilization obey one set of loyalties, ideals, code of honor and of economic values. That this code of values, customs, and ideals is not completely harmonized is emphatically stated in one of the principles, No. 4, of our table. But the code as a whole differs so profoundly from the African tribal codes in its economic and technical implications, in its political machinery nominally based on Christian principles but associated with our capitalist economy and imperialism, that it must be given a special place in our diagram and our argument. This European civilization, as expressed in our principle No. 3, plays also a different role in the whole process, in that it is the active and dynamic factor of change.

As regards African cultures, it is obviously not possible to treat them as one united system. The divergences between the Islamic communities of the Western Sudan, the Hottentots, Baganda, Bushmen, and Congo Pygmies are so considerable that to place them within one cultural category would stultify all generalization. Therefore in treating each area a special discussion will be necessary where we confront European impact with tribal response. But one fundamental fact remains: in each case we have to collate the Western influence with the special tribal culture. In this the anthropologist has to drive in the very elementary yet chronically neglected fact that in all attempts to deal with African humanity the European does not deal with a *tabula rasa*, with an indefinitely plastic material which can be used for purposes of uplift or labor, of taxes or moral improvements, without reference to its existing cultural constitution. The claim that tribal Africans obey a specific cultural determinism of their own means that to implant new habits in nutrition, or new methods in agriculture, or new statutes and law, we have to supersede certain cultural realities; and that if the process is carried out without consideration of the existing forces, it may lead simply to disorganization and conflict. The treatment of witchcraft and the simple-minded evangelization of the Natives; the tendency to educate the African without realizing what education destroys, and what it implies in matters of citizenship and opportunity; the conception of the *lobola* as a "savage custom of selling the bride," are one and all examples of the complete neglect by practical agents of the principle of African cultural determinism.

In our analysis of the vitality of African institutions, in our search for the reasons and causes thereof, we came to the conclusion that the old cultural order of Africa has been deeply affected, that it has in some cases been superseded by mere anarchy and disorder, but that wherever Africans, tribal or detribalized, live and thrive, the indigenous system of social, economic, and legal forces and values still remains a source of strength and inspiration to the African. Here again, the survival of the lobola in the most detribalized communities of South Africa, the fact that educated Africans are asking for chieftainship through the Transkeian Bunga, as well as the fact that the African has to rely on his own economic organization and resources for his livelihood and the social insurance for his unemployment—these examples themselves illustrate what is meant at this moment. We have argued that the African still has his cultural world and lives by its values and inspirations; first, because this is best adapted to his needs, having been evolved in the course of long history; secondly, because the selective giving of Europeans, that is, the withholding of some of the most desirable and valuable elements in our culture, and the principle of the industrial color bar and of tribal segregation throw back sections of the indigenous population on the resources of their own culture.[3] Glancing at our principles 7 and 8, we see that they correspond and sum up briefly this part of our argument, for which more examples and data will be found in the previous sections.

What is the cultural determinism of the African who lives in the no-man's-land of contact and change? The worker in the mines, the plantation hand, or the urbanized Native has not completely given up his tribal law, his customs, his kinship allegiances, and even his loyalties to the tribal authorities. But the hold which they have over him has been profoundly affected. He has not adopted the European outlook; he is by no means wholly subject to European cultural determinism. No human being can completely adopt a set of religious attitudes and values, unless he be allowed to be a full member of a religious congregation, without the spiritual color bar running athwart. No man follows a system of laws willingly and with full consent unless he can see and approve the principles of justice underlying them, and unless he enjoys the privileges inherent in the obligations. And it is equally impossible to become fully associated with an economic system in which most of the burdens are placed on one section alone and most privileges are withheld.

But in defining the cultural determinism of the African world of change and transition with the main aim of conceptual clarity and precision, we can say that this determinism results not from the "mixture" of European and African but rather from the working of the several guiding (or misguiding) principles of European policy and influence. The determinism is also deeply affected here by the rifts and inconsistencies within the European camp: that between missionary and entrepreneur on the one hand, and the *Realpolitik* of the settler policy, the Union laws, and the demands of economic enterprise on the other. It must also be remembered that all phenomena of change include not only Africans but also Europeans.

3. It should be noted that the principles of industrial color bar and of tribal segregation operate in the Union and to some extent in Southern Rhodesia, but not in Kenya, Tanganyika, Nigeria, and other parts of Africa.

Black and White always work together in the new institutions—that is, if we make an exception of certain new autonomous African movements. Change, therefore, presents a new type of culture, indeed, a new type highly dependent on the character of European impact but always embracing also the reaction of old tribal values and attitudes to this impact. The new laws which control contact and coöperation, the new political systems, the new types of economic enterprise are, as we have so often stressed, without precedent in either of the cultures. They are not to be understood by direct reference to any parent culture but must be studied as processes running on their own specific lines. This point gives the fieldworker engaged on contact study a role far more important than if the character of culture change could be diagnosed or foretold by the mere study of "borrowing" or "mixing." If, by the diagnosis of how much of European culture and how much of African enters into a mining enterprise or an African church or a Bantu school, we could foresee how these institutions would develop, there would be no need of careful and comprehensive observation of each special development.

As a matter of fact, the whole argument of this book contains one important moral of method. We have seen everywhere that a living process like that of culture change cannot be studied merely by documents and verbal utterances. A full knowledge of what culture change really means and what it looks like can only be acquired by the man and woman who have actually worked in the three fields which constitute African change. He must be at home with White policies, principles, and above all with the practice of the Whites in Africa. He must have acquired a firsthand knowledge of African modes of thought and behavior, through field work in a representative African area. He must also extend his field work to the typical and important phases of culture change—the Rand or the Copper Belt, plantations and schools, churches and law courts.

Some Remarks Concerning the Structural Features of the Diagram

So far we have discussed the principles in Table I. We must now turn to the chart and its uses. Its importance as well as its limitations will be best seen by a concrete application in the five cases which will be analyzed in the ensuing chapters. Here we shall content ourselves with only general remarks.

First and foremost, if the chart is all that is claimed for it, that is, a real help, its structural features must correspond to some realities.

The chart is a table of three main entries, of which the nature is already roughly evident. They express the threefold approach which has been agreed upon. How in principle and in practice are the dividing lines between A and B, and B and C, determined? Are they so hard and fast in reality as on paper? And what does the vertical division so neatly expressed in our scheme mean in real life?

Let us start at once from Column B, which has usually come last in all our discussion. Conceptually it is the most important, and indeed it occupies the central place in our chart, for after all change *is* the problem. In B we find the translation of A (of the European intentions, the benevolences and greeds of European impact) into practical action; and B, as we note, is sooner or later bound gradually to engulf and supersede the whole of C. *De facto*, C, as it exists now, is a by-product of B.[4] For the remaining forces and influences of tribalism are due first to the fact that the Europeans neither can nor wish to draw into their workshops of change the whole African population; secondly, to the fact that the discriminative and one-sided European impact not only attracts but repels; not only draws in the African but throws him back onto his tribal resources.

Now in these sentences we have already defined as precisely as it is necessary the two vertical lines. The distinction between the material which we list in A and that which we place in B must center round the question: is the given cultural feature (a law, an educational scheme, a hygienic reform, a constitution of Indirect Rule, or an administrative measure) still in the stage of European intention? That is, do we deal with a project, a plan, or a preparatory move on the part of the European population; or is that already a plan set in action, translated into a coöperative institution? As long as we deal with cultural facts devised exclusively by Europeans, and containing merely the moves of White administration, commercial bodies and settler communities, we have evidence belonging to our Column A.[5] Thus under A we would list such general principles of policy as the "White Man's Country"; the policies of European colonial ministries, whether it be Indirect Rule or full acculturation, the old predatory rule of the Congo area or the new constitution of Belgian politics, the colonial

---

4. Since the term "by-product" occurred in the original text, I have allowed it to stand here, although it seems to me to be likely to create misunderstanding. It is inconsistent with Malinowski's emphasis on the point that African culture has its own cultural determinism, its own sources of vitality. Hence the phrase that "C, as it exists now, is a by-product of B" can only be taken in the sense that the existing residue of African culture owes its form to the influences and modifications induced by B. Ed.

5. In A also belong of course institutions transported from Europe, though adapted to African conditions, that is, the White homestead, the White quarter of Johannesburg, banks, exchanges, etc.

ambitions of Fascism or the Hertzog Laws of the Union. Missionary policy; economic enterprise in so far as it takes the supply of cheap African labor for granted; the aims and ambitions of White settlers which have not gone beyond planning—all this is separated by the first line and placed under A.

The legitimacy of this procedure is warranted by the fact that a good deal of European planning happens as if Africans, with all their needs, their own economic pursuits, their love of independence, and their desire for self-expression, did not exist. Another justification for placing European intentions under A as a separate factor is, of course, due to the diversity of the separate agencies. When it comes to education, for instance, it is not enough only to list the views and plans of the protagonists of uplift, the pro-Natives, and the educational department. Native education in its various aspects is opposed by the White labor unions in South Africa; by the vested interests of capital, which prefer to deal with workers not readily accessible to propaganda; by the settler and by all this type of opinion which can be summed up under the eternal slogan, "Give me the raw Native every time." In questions of sexual morality, church attendance, and the springing up of independent African Christian churches, the missionary influence cannot be considered alone. We should also have to list the attitude of the Whites, which undermines missionary influence as soon as it is well under way. Otherwise half of the phenomena of change will not be explicable. All this has been stressed several times, but it must be remembered that this very fact makes column A indispensable, along with its development under several headings.

What would be the line of division between B and C? If we apply the above remarks, we can lay down with a certain measure of precision that wherever we have institutions or constitutional factors of organized work in which the White has achieved as integral a part as the Black, the phenomena must be registered under B. Such institutions as Native schools under White supervision, mines and plantations, mixed courts, systems of Indirect Administration and Native administration in general, would all figure in this column.

In Column C we should put all those phases of African life where the tradition of tribalism is the main determining factor of conduct, organization, and belief. Thus C does not refer merely to tribal areas. Its protagonist is not the raw African clad in skins or bark cloth, engaged in an act of witchcraft or hunting lions or leopards. Were we to apply our three-column approach to the urbanized Natives of Johannesburg, we would still have to list the influence of tribal tradition in all places where people recognize in principle or practice their membership in a tribe; speak their tribal language; render tribute or allegiance to a chief; marry under African tribal law; develop Bantu kinship bonds; believe openly or secretly in witchcraft; practice ancestor worship, and prefer Bantu beer even to whiskey. Thus, the line of distinction between B and C is equally well defined.

As we shall see in the following concrete analyses, the Muganda who nowadays owns his land under a new charter still obeys the biddings of the old form of land tenure—not always, but more often than not. And in most of his acts he is partly moved by the new interests of cash crops and monetary economy, and partly by old ideals and loyalties. We shall also see that while under Indirect Rule the chief assumes new functions derived from White intentions, the core of his authority is due to his traditional power, based on belief, ancestor cult, lineage, and memories of the historical past. Here again, even in discussions of a single line of behavior, we can separate these factors from those pertaining to A, and show how the interaction produces B. The line of division between B and C is as clear as that between A and B.

It might appear that we have gone very near to that analysis of culture which corresponds to the concept of "mixture" and "borrowing." To a certain extent this is true, but such a view is entirely superficial and leads us to make two fundamental corrections. The analysis and disentanglement of the active forces are necessary; but first of all, as we have seen, European culture is not just a heap of opportunities from which the African can take whatever he likes. Under Column A we do not list European culture as a treasure house of goods, values, and benefactions from which anything might be taken to effect the mixture. European culture faces, or rather attacks, the African as a well-organized body of interests, or more correctly as a number of organized interests, each oriented on its own lines, each acting for a definite purpose and giving only as much and not more than lies in its system of vested interests. And all those interests, let us remember, are by no means coördinated, harmonized, or unified. The second correction that we have to make is that Column B is by no means a mechanical compound, or a direct product of the mixture of A and C. The manner in which impact from A and the reaction from C takes place will appear under B. This must be definitely observed, empirically ascertained, and not deduced from factors in A and in C.

PART TWO

VIII

AFRICAN WARFARE

HAVING formulated the methods and principles which are necessary for the study of culture change, we may now apply them to some specific African institutions. Let us consider indigenous African warfare. The organization of many African tribes from the Sudan down to Pondoland was connected with chieftainship, and through the chief as war lord, with the military activities of the tribe. Age grades, the religious character of leadership, war magic, regimentation, even marriage and family life were determined by the fact that the young unmarried men had to take part in more or less regular military expeditions. Some of these were wars of conquest but usually they were merely raids for slaves, cattle, or loot.

Here we deal with a phenomenon of purely African character. The first action of European influence, missionary, administrative, and economic, is to stop fighting completely and remove the causes of war as well as the organization for war. Apparently then we have to deal with a factor completely wiped off the slate so far as present African conditions are concerned. We have also a situation in which the only possible contribution of the anthropologist would seem to be a reconstruction of the past and a comparison of this with the present. Yet it is clear at once that such a comparison could contribute no criteria of guidance and would be of no practical value whatsoever. For the fact is that whatever functions, useful or deleterious, organizing or destructive, African war might have filled in the past, none of them are possible in the present, nor could we envisage their revival in the future. On the one hand, the European, rightly or wrongly, registers African war in Africa as completely immoral, though he cannot apply the same point of view to his own affairs in Europe. On the other, and this is even more important, European occupation has practically abolished slavery and large-scale cattle lifting; has obliterated the old tribal hostilities; and has done away with the independence and sovereignty of African kingdoms and tribes. The only thing which can be said about the past of indigenous warfare is that it is dead as regards all those conditions which produced it, maintained it, and allowed it to bring about certain organizing, as well as destructive, effects.

Would it be true, however, to say that the tradition of the old military pursuits is completely dead in any African tribe? First of all, it is a well-known fact that even where indigenous authority and chieftainship have been entirely disregarded by the administrative machinery of Europeans, it is not dead to the African. When Indirect Rule was imposed upon former German East African colonies, there was no difficulty anywhere in finding the legitimate chiefs or in reestablishing their power. When in 1929 Northern Rhodesia followed suit, the institution of chieftainship, completely ignored and constitutionally obliterated for some thirty years, arose again strong, effective, and serviceable. The most Europeanized council of the Africans, the Bunga of the Transkei, has again and again passed "resolutions asking the government to consider the status of hereditary chiefs in the Transkei." [1] They did this, arguing that hereditary chieftainship means respect for authority in every way, even for that of the parents in the home, and hence is necessary for the reintegration of family life. The Report of the Native Economic Commission for South Africa (1930–32) tells us that the reverence for the chief and his family is ". . . a quality deeply ingrained in the Bantu. A number of educated natives who have never been ruled by chiefs pleaded very strongly . . . for some measure of restoration of the authority of the chiefs." [2]

To the African, the chief was the spiritual representative and high priest of the tribe; he was the supreme judge, and also the war lord. The traditions of the old glory, power, and independence are not dead. Dr. Hunter, in her analysis of war in Pondoland, shows clearly how strong is the living memory of present-day Pondo with regard to the past glories of the tribe and the power of the chief. It is still possible to ascertain the organization of the army and the elements of leadership; it is even possible to obtain elaborate details of the tribal rites practiced to maintain the strength, courage, and immunity of the soldiers.[3] First of all, we note that the anthropologist was able to reconstruct from the memory of living men the ethnography of war. As a tradition, the past of indigenous warfare is by no means dead, and

1. Hunter, *Reaction to Conquest*, p. 430.
2. Report of the Native Economic Commission, 1930–32, par. 35.
3. Hunter, *op. cit.*, pp. 400–413.

there is no need to reconstruct in any other sense than that of investigating a still extant oral piece of tribal knowledge and its present influence on the prestige, value, and importance of chieftainship. Nor is the institutionalized aspect completely obliterated. A great deal of the social organization which existed originally for the carrying out of war is still there and the chiefs, sub-chiefs, and captains perform some of their old duties—administrative, judicial, and religious—in virtue of their traditional hereditary position as war leaders. During a brief stay in Swaziland, where chieftainship and military organization are not dissimilar to that of the Pondo, I was able to see the old regiments and appreciate their new functions. They act today as important educational agencies, large labor camps, and indispensable elements in the magic and ritual which are inseparable from the very essence of tribal authority, chieftainship, and even domestic organization of the Swazi.

How far does this affect the European side of the question? Wherever the administration makes an attempt to utilize Native institutions, in this case chieftainship and the tribal framework of indigenous organization, it has to count with these traditional forces which still survive. And here the distinction between living and dead history is essential: between, on the one hand, all that has vanished with changed conditions; and, on the other hand, the institutions which still remain, and the sentiments from the past which continue as active forces today. For obviously certain aspects which have naturally and completely dropped out need not be dragged in or even considered: aspects such as slave raiding, mutilation, collective thieving, or the disposition of war booty. Only in so far as the memories of these activities still linger and in so far as they give certain tribes a feeling of aristocratic superiority over the others must they be taken into account. This distinction is important, even in our own highly advanced community. Popular tradition of past events is completely different from a scientific historical reconstruction. In Africa this also applies. Tribal pride, with all the mythology and historical legends which buttress it, is an active force still at work. The hard facts of past happenings, which in some cases can still be reconstructed laboriously by the anthropologist, are of interest only in so far as they establish divergence between mythology and history.[4]

We can, in order to bring out clearly some of the points of the argument, project our analysis of the problem of war in present-day

4. For another example of how far the living tradition produces a differential nationalism, separating the conquerors from the conquered, see Dr. Read's "Tradition and Prestige among the Ngoni," *Africa*, Vol. IX, No. 4 (1936).

changing Africa onto a synoptic chart (pp. 88–89).[5] Let us start with Column A, a definition of European policies, principles, and laws. The obvious thing to write down as our first entry is European conquest and political control. As A2, under the benefits of civilized rule, we should list "peace," in so far as there is an abolition of indigenous warfare through complete or partial disarmament. On the other hand, we must not forget that within the last quarter of a century Africa has been drawn by Europeans into a devastating war, in which Africans fought Africans without any quarrel, benefit, and, in the last issue, without any purpose whatsoever—for the fate of the war did not depend on the blood spilled in the Dark Continent. We cannot forget the cruelties and massacres of the last Abyssinian campaign, in which Europeans did not bring peace but a war fought in a manner far more destructive and barbarous than anything indigenously African. Therefore, side by side with "Abolition of indigenous warfare," we shall enter "Spread (or extension) of European world wars into Africa" (A3). We should also have to add "European use of African man power abroad," for the sending of Africans as fighters or as an army of occupation into some districts of Europe has produced far-reaching effects, in many ways adverse to the Africans as a race, and also dangerous for the future peace and good understanding of the world as a whole.[6]

As a corollary of these entries, and with reference to the wider establishment of peace, we should have to enter the disregard of indigenous military organization; the prohibition of the sale of arms to Natives; punitive expeditions; and the air bombing of peaceful villages (A2). Finally, under A4 we must write down "European moral doctrines—Christian, educational, and communistic—of war." Here we deal in Africa with the same phenomenon as at home, namely, the deep conflict between ideals and practice, between the protestations of universal brotherhood and their complete subordination to the demands of a "just and lawful war."

What corresponds to these entries in our second column, B? For B1 we have the new political system as affected by the loss of military sovereignty of the African tribe or monarchy; and the resultant changes in tribal relations and tribal organization. Along with this there may be a development of new military forces of a mixed African

5. Entries in the chart are referred to in the text by the letter of the column and a numeral, both placed in parentheses. Ed.

6. France has employed colonial troops outside of Africa, for instance, the Senegalese in the Ruhr occupation, and the Malagasy troops in the Druse revolt in Syria. West African troops also serve their term of conscription in France. *Vide* Mair, *Native Policies in Africa*, pp. 186–187.

SYNOPTIC CHART FOR THE STUDY OF AFRICAN WARFARE

A	B	C	D	E
WHITE INFLUENCES, INTERESTS, AND INTENTIONS	PROCESSES OF CULTURE CONTACT AND CHANGE	SURVIVING FORMS OF TRADITION	RECONSTRUCTED PAST	NEW FORCES OF SPONTANEOUS AFRICAN REINTEGRATION OR REACTION
1. European conquest and political control.	1. The new political system as affected by loss of military sovereignty of the African tribe or monarchy, and resultant changes in tribal organization. New military forces, of mixed African and European character.	1. African resistance and political submission in tribal memory and reaction.	1. African war in intertribal conditions (economic and political).	
2. Peace (abolition of indigenous warfare; complete disarmament; partial disarmament); European system of preventive control, of punitive expeditions; disregard of indigenous military organization.	2. More or less effective working of this control by mixed European and African police and military forces. European acceptance and coöperative control in residual activities. Decay of institutions, pursuits, and revenue directly dependent on war.	2. Living memory of past glory, romance, advantages of war. Residual activities of old fighting organizations (educative, economic, ceremonial) as institutionalized.	2. Position of chief as war leader, commander, war magician, and distributor of loot and booty.	
3. Spread (or extension) of European	3. Influence, political, economic and	3. Residual reactions from military en-	3. Traditional methods of warfare: strat-	3. African attitudes toward European

A	B	C	D	E
WHITE INFLUENCES, INTERESTS, AND INTENTIONS	PROCESSES OF CULTURE CONTACT AND CHANGE	SURVIVING FORMS OF TRADITION	RECONSTRUCTED PAST	NEW FORCES OF SPONTANEOUS AFRICAN REINTEGRATION OR REACTION
world wars into Africa. Use of African manpower, organized into European *cadres*.	social, of African military units on tribal life. African realization that war is accepted by Europeans. Disappearance of European inviolability; hence undermining of prestige.	terprise; or passive submission to recruitment.	egy, tactics, causes and effects.	powers, critical comparisons. Influence of White-made wars on indigenous nationalism.
4. European moral doctrines (Christian, educational, and communistic) and war.	4. Conflicts (intellectual, moral, and political) due to African discovery of European inconsistencies.	4. African ideals of bravery and value of war.	4. Principles of intertribal law in war and peace. Direct advantages: slavery, loot, tribute. Political effects on intertribal organization and conquest.	4. African reactions against Christianity and Western civilization.

and European character. The peremptory abolition of indigenous fighting (A2) has led to the decay of certain institutions, pursuits, and revenues which were derived from war (B2). This entry is merely negative, but it would raise such questions as how far certain personal values of honor and virility, of responsibility, of power, and of leadership have been affected by this. After all, we deal with these problems differently in Africa than in Europe. At home, we still regard war as a source of many personal and communal qualities which we are loath to sacrifice to the ideal of world peace. This is a problem which the fieldworker must face.[7]

7. This entry would also link up with its corresponding point in the scheme for the study of tribal authority, for obviously the complete suppression of the chief's powers as war leader has deprived him of a great deal of his authority, his revenue, and per-

What corresponds in Africa today to the third entry of A, that is, the fighting introduced directly by Europeans into Africa? We should have to consider here the influence—political, economic, and social—of African military units on tribal life; the realization that Europe is as divided as Africa; that war is accepted by Europeans; and with all this the disappearance of European inviolability, and hence the undermining of European prestige (B3). To the European disregard of African military organization (A2), there obviously corresponds a vast set of problems, which might be described as the re-adaptation of age grades, regiments, and other Native fighting units to functions countenanced by the administration: such functions as are educational, economic, political, and ceremonial. Some of these are still the old functions carried out side by side with fighting in past days; others have assumed a new importance and a new character. We could therefore enter under B2, "European acceptance and coöperative control in residual activities of the old fighting organization." Needless to say, all these items would have to be studied by the anthropologist as relevant factors in the social situation, and without any political bias, prejudice, or trend.

In passing to the "Surviving Forms of Tradition," as we have labeled Column C, we shall have to note African resistance and political submission, and the influence of these on present-day memory and reaction (C1). We shall have to list against the decay of military institutions (B2) the living memory of the past glory, romance, and advantages of war, such as described above among the Bemba, Pondo, and Ngoni (C2); while in C4 we should place African ideals of bravery and of the value of war. In the study of the old *cadres* as they survive, we should enter those activities and functions of which no official cognizance has been taken by European agencies: these are the phenomena of Column C which are not recognized in Column A; they are the vital African interests and institutions which are ignored in the framing of European policies. The comparison between this entry (C2) and 2 in Column B would show us how far under Indirect Rule and other systems which aim at adapting African life to the new requirements, use has been made of the old regiments. Quite recently, for instance, the National School of Swaziland has been reconstituted by adopting the old regimental principles in its class work.[8]

sonal prestige. And here perhaps, as in previous problems, one could think of suggestions for substitute factors and influences in order to buttress an institution which is not only a vital force in tribal life but essential to the Europeans under Indirect Rule.

8. For a detailed description of this see Hilda Beemer, "The Development of the Military Organization in Swaziland," *Africa*, X (1937), 195–203.

This fact would obviously be entered, as already indicated, under Column B, but the inculcating of loyalty to the chief, the teaching of tribal traditions, and the training in sexual morality, which for years have been carried on in the old regimental camps without any co-operation or recognition by missionary, educationalist, and governmental official, belong to Column C. Finally, corresponding to the spread of European wars (A3), we should have to study in Column C the residual reactions from military enterprise or the passive submission to recruitment.

To the anthropologist who tries to organize his material in a way useful both theoretically and practically, the division here advocated is the only suitable one. It allows us to distribute the material directly with reference to the fundamental fact that on certain points Africa and Europe coöperate and on others work quite independently. The anthropologist might on this basis offer some further suggestions and criticism. Much of the economic work done by the regiments in Swaziland is of public utility. Considering the delicate question of forced labor and the constant tendency of the administration to encroach on the privileges of the chief, the fieldworker ought to bring out the distinction between public works of tribal importance and work done primarily or exclusively for the individual benefit of the chief. I think a careful study of the subject would show that very little is done for the private advantage of the ruler and that most of the work is done for ends of public utility.

Looking again at our synoptic chart, we should list in Column D, the reconstructed past, such phenomena as the intertribal conditions of an area: for instance, the existence of aggressive and efficient tribes side by side with economically effective agricultural communities. Cattle raiding was, for the Masai and for most other Hamitic and Nilotic tribes, one of their main sources of income. Interesting as this is from the point of view of human relations past and present, it cannot yield any practical guidance for the future, for we cannot revive or encourage stealing. Here too must be entered the position of the chief as war leader (D2), not in the way in which this affects his prestige nowadays but rather as an actual instrument of power, in that he was commander, chief magician, and distributor of war booty. Again, these past conditions, as they actually existed, are of no relevance whatsoever, though the memory of them may still contribute to the maintenance of the chief's status. In so far as they accomplish this, they constitute data for Column C. Finally, we should need a full description of the causes and effects of warfare, methods, strategy, and tactics (D3), together with an account of the principles of intertribal law in peace and war (D4), for these to the comparative student of human warfare are of great interest.[9] To the administrator and applied anthropologist such knowledge is irrelevant since large-scale fighting has been completely suppressed by European occupation.

If we turn to Column E, new forces of spontaneous African reintegration or reaction, we should have to note that as a result of the spread of European wars to Africa (A3) an incentive has been given to the African to compare and criticize various European nations, and this has had its effect on indigenous nationalism and has led to demands for independence and self-determination (E3).

Our study of warfare has enabled us to detect and classify the forces operative in culture contact. Even in the discussion of a phenomenon which is relegated to the past, we see that the only relevant element from the practical point of view is its survival in a subterranean and partly mutilated form in present-day life. The comparative survey in which the various approaches have been treated separately and yet correlated at every step would, I think, be as valuable an instrument in actual field work as it is suggestive in drawing conclusions and in the condensed tabulation of results. It suggests specific points of detail for careful investigation in each area, and also allows us to formulate certain conclusions for general statesmanship. With regard to warfare, the moral reflection with the widest importance is whether, boasting as we do that we have given the African peace fully and forever, we are not really camouflaging a crime of the first magnitude by drawing African tribesmen into our armed quarrels, with their wholesale destruction of life and property.[10] Would not one of the first steps on the road to peace consist in agreeing once and for all that the colonies should not be drawn as actual fighting units into European wars?

9. For a comparative discussion of war and its relevance for modern European conditions, see Malinowski, "An Anthropological Analysis of War," *American Journal of Sociology*, XLVI, No. 4, 521–550. Ed.

10. This manuscript was written by Malinowski between 1938 and 1939. What his attitude would have been to the use of Native troops in the present war, I do not know; but certainly the "European gift of peace" to the so-called primitive peoples who have been forced to submit to administration by the more "civilized" nations has acquired an even greater irony. Ed.

Among Malinowski's papers there were some notes on Dr. Hunter's material on war in Pondoland. He considered that some points in particular required detailed investigation, namely, whether the Natives believe that, with the cessation of tribal hostilities, the virility of the men has suffered; whether in fact there are symptoms of decay; whether internal fighting has increased in volume in the tribe; whether there are other types of compensatory exercises, such as cattle raiding by stealth, etc. "What is really important for the present and future," he stressed, "is how far the destruction of military organization has undermined authority, certain personal and emotional qualities; how far it has released energies for different types of pursuits." Ed.

It seems a foregone conclusion that when there is war in Europe no amount of bloodshed by Africans in Africa will contribute to the final settlement of these issues. Why then organize the Africans for bigger and bloodier wars, if one of the unquestionable benefits which we could give them would be real peace?

IX

REFLECTIONS ON WITCHCRAFT

THERE is no doubt that all efforts of European missionaries, education-alists, and administrators have failed until now in their treatment of witchcraft. We find everywhere reports that it is on the increase: [1] Orde-Browne states that the handling of the problem is the least satis-factory part of the administration; [2] while the tremendous sway of such witch-finding organizations as the *Bamuchapi* shows how power-ful the belief is. The valuable argument adduced by Dr. Richards in her article on the Bemba indicates how disintegration, if it removes certain beliefs, also increases those in witchcraft. [3] Here we have a typical problem of culture change: one of the most characteristic of African superstitions and symptoms of benightedness not decreasing but becoming stronger under the enlightened influence of mission teaching and education. Wherever the student finds these paradoxical results, he ought very definitely to signal them, to reveal causation, and if he sees any possibilities of advice, he ought to give it. The coura-geous stand taken by Frank Melland, an ex-government administrator, puts many anthropologists to shame. [4]

Here if anywhere there should be perfect collaboration on the one common factor on which both sides, European and African, seem to meet, and indeed ought to meet—that is, the eradication of witchcraft. The administrator, the missionary, the educationalist, and even the entrepreneur to whom the alleged witch doctor may be a disturbing force among Native labor—all are at one in wishing to stamp it out. This coincides completely with the wholehearted desire of the Afri-can to have sorcery extirpated. Why have we then the paradox that it persists, even while Europeans fight against it and punish for it, and the Africans suffer under it? The latter demand nothing more than to be rid of what they regard as a dangerous and criminal force. And yet it is here that we find in the actual handling of the matter almost complete divergence between the joint aims of Native and European alike on the one hand, and the results obtained on the other.

1. A special number of *Africa* was devoted to a discussion of witchcraft. In addition to the other writers mentioned throughout this chapter, see also the article by C. Clifton Roberts, "Witchcraft and Colonial Legislation," *Africa*, Vol. VIII (1935).

2. G. St. J. Orde-Browne, "Witchcraft and British Colonial Law," *Africa*, VIII, 483.

3. A. I. Richards, "A Modern Movement of Witch-Finders," VIII, 458.

4. F. Melland, "Ethical and Political Aspects of African Witchcraft," *Africa*, VIII, 495–503.

Witchcraft, abhorred by the African, and proscribed by the European, has been driven from open recognition, but it is practiced in a clandestine manner, apparently to an even larger extent than in the olden days. It is reported to flourish in the mine compounds, the urban locations, plantations, and even mission stations. The reasons seem to me not far to seek. In devising means to rid the Africans from the scourge, the Europeans proceeded without even an adequate knowledge of the facts or an intelligent handling of principles. A state of mind which is deeply rooted and founded, not in accidental superstition but in universal human psychology, cannot be abolished by legislation. It cannot be eradicated by mere nonrecognition and denial of its existence.

What has been the European approach? The European is tempted both to underrate and to exaggerate the belief. As a skeptic, enlightened and Christian, he discounts its possibility, and in this he is undoubtedly correct. As a benevolent and paternal ruler, he cannot help being impressed by the strength of the primitive belief; by the blackmail element in it; the unhappiness which it causes; the hate and resentment which go with it. Hence he is moved both by the conviction that it is a figment and by the realization that it is a dangerous figment. He therefore legislates against its practice, which, if it be a reality, should not be ignored by legal decree! He also legislates against accusation of witchcraft, thus punishing criminal and detective alike! The nonsensical element lies in the fact that in the Northern Rhodesian statute, for example, equal penalty attaches to the practicing of witchcraft (a) and to the accusing of witchcraft (b). Yet if (a) is a crime, how can you prosecute those who bear witness against those practicing witchcraft? If (b) is a crime, then (a) cannot be one. In other words to realize one half of the code you have to stultify the other, or else you have to jail the accused and the accuser always in couples.

What is the reality at the bottom of witchcraft? The answer to this, and only a correct answer, can disclose the common factor. We can take our stand on the principle that you cannot kill by witchcraft. At the same time, equally strongly, we must insist that the belief in sorcery is psychologically effective. On the one hand it undermines the vitality of the patient; it hampers his action; and so ultimately may contribute to his death. The whole modern psychiatric approach, Coué, faith healing, Christian Science, in so far as they have any element of therapeutic effectiveness, prove that the mental diathesis of the patient is of the greatest importance. Allow the sick man to feel that his sickness is being manufactured, give a man the belief that a run of ill luck has been started against him, and he may succumb.

But even this explanation points only to the effects of the belief and not to the psychological, social, and economic foundations of its persistence. Witchcraft is not primarily founded on the aggressive malice of the sorcerer, who wishes to do harm and who blackmails his victims into the belief in it. The sorcerer is often the unwilling, sometimes the conniving, victim. Witchcraft is primarily rooted in the psychological reactions of those suffering from ill health, misfortune, inability to control their destiny and fortunes. As such, it is a translation of destiny and of personal mishap due to the rulings of fate, into terms of manageable human malice. It is thus a theory constructed *post hoc,* to account for ill luck, disease, and death. It is an agency in which the initiative, the ill will, and the active procedure are imputed to definite human beings. The diagnosis is given sometimes by direct revelation, dreams, visions, but usually by diviners. Then proceedings can be taken. The witch is accused, tried, made to undo the harm, or counter-magic may be employed. To free human beings from the belief in sorcery, it would be necessary to endow them with gifts of eternal prosperity, health, and life.

There are thus two fundamental principles on which black magic is based. One of them, to blame a human being for misfortune, reduces the metaphysical or fatalistic elements in one's reaction to it. There is more hope in counteracting human machinations than in dealing with decrees of fate or the will of God. From this point of view, once we understand the psychological, social, and moral roots, we see that witchcraft, far from being an unmitigated evil, is in many ways a source of comfort and hope; a handle to manage the unmanageable. In so far as a belief in black magic always implies the belief in countering it, it may sometimes through the same psychological channels save the patient. The eternal slogan of the missionary, the uplifter, or the educationalist: "We free these people from the incubus of witchcraft," is therefore only half a truth; in fact it covers the lesser half.

The other essential component of black magic is sociological. What are the social and personal determinants which allow the blame to be fixed on one individual rather than another? Since witchcraft is based on the scapegoat psychology, the most likely people to be blamed are those with whom conflict most readily occurs. Thus some personal characteristics predestine to the role of sorcerer or witch, unbalanced individuals, exceptionally gifted ones, people with abnormalities, physical or mental. Within certain social relationships, suspicion is also determined on more general lines. Sometimes those blamed are among the nearest kinsmen or relatives-in-law, as might be expected from the sound residuum of psychoanalysis, which every man of science can accept as well founded. Or again, witchcraft is often suspected in relationships of considerable social or economic stress; or the suspicion may flourish between people who have been engaged in some conflict, legal, economic, or political.

The belief in witchcraft will always remain a symptom of economic distress, of social tension, of political or social oppression. We have only to look at the present conditions in Europe [4a] and see how the scapegoat psychology has given rise to attitudes and actions essentially akin to witch hunting: the persecution of Jews in Germany; of saboteurs, spies, and Trotskyists in Russia; and of liberals and anti-Fascists in Italy. Such a psychology is universally human and persistent: I mean the concentration of blame and hatred on certain clearly defined groups suspected of causing evils for which one otherwise would have to blame all the members of the community, its government, the decrees of destiny, or other elements against which immediate reaction is not possible. In Africa, culture change produces, on the whole, conditions of economic distress, political unrest, and personal conflicts. No wonder therefore that the belief in witchcraft increases rather than abates.

Now I submit that the common measure between the rational and logical approach to witchcraft and Native belief must be looked for in the sociological context of human malice, competition, and sense of injury, which form the actual framework in social relationships, upon which the supernatural power has always to work. Suppose A believes that he is bewitched and accuses B of witchcraft. This accusation may mean that B, who is a strong personality, has been systematically persecuting A, and that the supernatural act is but part of his whole network of malicious overt practices. Or it may mean the reverse: that B has injured A in a way not actionable in European or Native courts. The natural thing to do, one equally useful from the European and the Native point of view, would be to drag out an accusation, to treat it on its psychological merits, and to allow the case to come before a supervised Native court.[5] It would thus reveal the framework of malpractices, of malicious acts and counter-acts, of intrigues and hatreds. I do not mean to imply by any means that this would be a perfect solution. It might be at times a case of public catharsis, almost in the psychoanalytic sense. At times it might bring to light certain actual and actionable malpractices carried out in the relationship between A and B, and possibly directed as from the bewitched against the wizard. In such cases witchcraft is merely the

4a. 1938. Ed.
5. A strong advocate of treating witchcraft seriously is the above-mentioned Frank Melland. For a statement of his position see his article, *op. cit.*, pp. 502–503.

CHART OF WITCHCRAFT CRITICISM

A	B	C
WHITE INFLUENCES, INTERESTS, AND INTENTIONS	PROCESSES OF CULTURE CONTACT AND CHANGE	SURVIVING FORMS OF TRADITION
1. Sincere desire to stamp out witchcraft.	1. The common factor: apparent ideal of sympathetic collaboration between Native informants and enlightened inquirer.	1. Wholehearted anxiety to be rid of witchcraft.
2. Summary proscription of belief in magic: undiscriminating, rigid, sweeping, and uninformed.	2. Driven underground, it flourishes under conditions of change in towns and locations as much as on reserves. Complete bewilderment. Impression that European law abets sorcery. Strong resentment.	2. Firm belief still survives in: good and bad magic; sorcery with intent to harm; and countermagic which antidotes it.
3. Ignorance of the real psychological and social mechanisms. Present legislation implies: a) principle that state of of mind or belief can be overcome by political methods; b) conviction that sorcery though an illusion is yet an evil; c) it fails to introduce this essential distinction.	3. Natives register increase in witchcraft and sorcery. Blame European, missionary, and administration for it. Real cause: increase in misery, ill health, impossibility of controlling poverty; paralleled by increasing rivalries among the Natives.	3. Belief based on powerful foundations due to: a) psychological and cultural reality of magic. Translation of Fate into malice; b) psychology of translation of determinism of Fate into human or supernatural; scapegoat psychology; c) the limited but real service rendered by witchcraft to individual or community in distress.
4. Slackness in practice and difficulties of administration in understanding and applying. Attitude of missions who partly ignore, partly oppose belief as a whole.	4. Indigenous movements of witch hunting (*Bamuchapi*), using elements of new methods against background of old belief. Their temporary success —an index of vitality of (A).	4. Old type of witch finding undermined by administrative persecution. Unable to cope with new suspicions leveled against Christian Natives.

weaker man's only retaliation. Some legal action, giving satisfaction to the victim of the previous malpractice, might at the same time remove a latent but real injustice and equally do away with the fear of supernatural vengeance. In any case it would allow the European code of law not to drive practices of and belief in witchcraft underground, nor to give the Natives the feeling that they have been delivered into the hands of all the black magicians that be. And it might, I venture to say, lead to the airing of a great many grievances which in some instances might be capable of real redress.

Here then the anthropologist suggests a number of practical conclusions from his argument. First and foremost, it would be well not to deny the reality of witchcraft, but to acknowledge it as a fact, thus establishing the common measure of mutual understanding between the African and the European. Since not all cases of witchcraft are the by-product of actual oppression, injustice, or exploitation, the permission to discuss accusations of witchcraft before a Native court might lead to an indirect remedy. Again, and above all, to treat that symptom of general maladjustment in any other way than by creating better economic, political, and legal conditions is obviously preposterous.

Here once more practical anthropology leads us to the reframing of problems, to the posing of new questions, and to an analysis which is at the same time wider, more comprehensive, more genuinely functional and capable of practical application.[6]

---

6. While education may operate as one factor in decreasing the belief in witchcraft, in my opinion it plays a far lesser part than is usually assumed. No amount of education has helped to prevent modern forms of witch hunting in Germany, Russia, and Italy. In this instance, prosperity may be of greater value than wisdom.

(In Malinowski's manuscripts on witchcraft, the problems are obviously handled in terms of his three-column approach, but there are no direct references to a chart. He had, however, drawn up several charts, and among these, two incorporated the various points taken up in this chapter. I have therefore included one here as a summary of evidence and argument in the preceding section. Ed.)

X

PROBLEMS OF NATIVE DIET IN THEIR
ECONOMIC SETTING

LET us now turn to a subject which is as much a question of the present and future as indigenous warfare is a thing of the past. The diet and commissariat of African tribes have been very much affected by the change in economic conditions; and planning, research, and policy as regards diet must therefore be inspired by present-day conditions in tribal areas and by future outlook rather than by an antiquarian interest in the oddities of the past. There are some specific questions of nutrition which belong to the field of contact and change: the large-scale feeding of Native labor; the attempts to introduce new crops; the development of new tastes and new dietetic habits. That such phenomena have to be considered in relation to the nutritive habits of the tribal Natives who are drafted into labor camps or mine compounds, who work on plantations or in coöperation with the Whites as employees, is evident. At the same time, the change is largely produced and controlled by European influence. Matters are also complicated by the fact that the various European agencies and interests are not working as a unit, or even with a well-balanced and correlated policy. Within the administrative control the political official, the medical expert and the administrator, the officer of medical services and the educationalist work at times without careful coördination of their aims and methods. Again, the practice of large-scale European enterprise, although often submitting to government rules, is mainly determined by its own economic requirements and limitations. When, as in South Africa and in the Belgian Congo, it has at its service a body of scientific experts who plan a rational system of dietetics, this specific form of European influence must also be considered a factor in the situation.

Recently there have been several attempts to approach the subject of African diet from the scientific side. It is realized that new strains, muscular and nervous, have been put upon the African; that he is exposed to new types of illness, and that he often works under conditions less hygienic than those of his tribal existence. In order to maintain the health of the Native, to raise his working efficiency and even his general standard of energy, intelligence, and resistance to disease, research and practical rules resulting from it are necessary. It is recognized by the biologists and medical men working on the problem that to deal with disease without consideration of preventive measures and a constructive scheme of nutrition is futile, and also that a "continuous supply of sufficient and well-balanced food" depends "on the economic status of the community." [1] The study of changing diet must therefore bring in the anthropologist as the collaborator of the physician and biologist, since at all points the nutritive needs of the African must be examined in relation to his changing environment, economic, political, and social.

It is clear from these preliminary remarks that we can best map out the problem by using our synoptic scheme embodying the threefold approach. We can see, in regard to this subject also, the irrelevance of the historical zero point, that is, the tribal conditions as they existed before the advent of Europeans. Whether the ancestors of the laborers in a mining compound have been cannibals or vegetarians, whether they throve on large herds of cattle or starved in a desert area matters nothing to the dietitian determining calories, vitamin content, and food values. On the other hand, it matters very much whether these Natives come from slum yards or have been recruited in reserves where the tribal commissariat still survives to a large extent in its pristine form. It matters very much whether they come to their work and to their meals accustomed to European diet or with tastes, food habits, and prejudices broken down, pandered to, or re-adapted.

Take a child in a slum of Johannesburg, Pretoria, or Durban. Whether it is starved or overfed depends on the income of its parents, on the supply of food available, and on the formation of its habits. The knowledge of how much the town Native has retained of the old traditional needs and ideas; the existence of meat feasts connected with ritual killings tacked on from ancient times to Christian ceremonies; the Bantu preferences for mealie as against wheat—all this is significant theoretically and important practically. But the behavior of his great-grandparents in hunting and agriculture, in feeding and feasting, is irrelevant to any plan for dietetic improvement. The Africans from the south, west, east, or center of the continent now have entirely different and new resources at their disposal. On the other hand, they have been deprived of some of their previous assets and greatly restricted in the carrying out of their earlier occupations. Nothing will restore that healthy, evidently palatable supply of food

1. These are conclusions reached at the International Conference on the Health Services, held at Cape Town, 1932. Quoted in the volume of *Africa* devoted to problems of nutrition, IX, No. 2, 153. We shall have an opportunity to return to this important collection of essays on African diet under conditions of culture contact.

connected with cannibalism. Slave labor is no longer available for planned improvements in agriculture. The plough is now an element in the tilling of the soil. Above all, however, no program can intelligently hark back to times when no money economy existed in Africa, when no large quantities of foodstuffs from abroad could be marketed in the tribal areas, and when the Natives had nothing to give in exchange for imported food. The entry of Africa into world economy has swept clean off the slate of relevant and vital facts a great many of the old conditions which formerly affected Native diet.

These old conditions will never return again in their integral pristine form. At the same time, the main types of African economy are still tribal; and their nutritive habits, their gastronomic predilections, their devotion to indigenous beer, and their attitudes toward meat and cattle are still powerful forces in matters of income and food, and a strong social and psychological influence. To distinguish between what is dead and buried in the past and what still strongly survives is, in the question of diet, obviously of primary importance. This can only be achieved by separating historical reconstruction, with all its specific methods of observation and dialectics, from the simple and direct observation of the institutions, traditions, and values which still obtain.

It is well to register here that the Nutrition Committee of the International African Institute has fully recognized this principle. In their statement of the problem,[2] the reconstructed past does not figure at all, and the questions refer to the types of food now consumed and produced, to the effects of this new diet, and to the determinants of the Natives' choice of food. The statement could not be better, but it is more useful to consider the factors at work under the three headings of European influence, actual processes of change, and tribal strongholds of tradition, rather than lumped together under a single heading.

In Column A of the synoptic scheme (pp. 104–105) we place as usual White influences, interests, and intentions. The method of study here, of course, would be based on field work among the Whites who control Native nutrition, including the research workers in biology, medicine, and social conditions; the directors of mine compounds and locations, and also the traders who sell food to the Natives. It would involve the perusal of the available documents and an acquaintance with the theories and policies of government departments, missionaries, and entrepreneurs. But here, as always, the White intentions can never be simply translated into practice. Take, for example, scientific

2. *Loc. cit.,* p. 148.

advice on feedin The pioneer work of Drs. Orr and Gilks has revealed highly in   sting facts concerning two representative tribes,
the Masai who su   it mostly on meat, blood, and milk; and the Kikuyu
who rely on a ve   able diet. These two types of nutrition have been
correlated with t   physical characteristics, the resistance to disease,
and even the gen al efficiency of the tribes.[3] But it is clear that such
knowledge cann t be directly translated into practice. However
clearly we recognize that the Masai need more gruel and the Kikuyu
more steak, we cannot spoon-feed the former nor fork-feed the latter.
The difficulty of the commissariat on a tribal scale is obviously insur-
mountable, and apart from this there would be the additional problem
of re-forming their tastes. The Masai, through the age-long formation
of their habits, have developed a cultural attitude which makes them
simply dislike vegetable food and despise agriculture. The Kikuyu
object equally to an excessive diet of meat, though from time to time
they like to gorge on a slaughtered animal. You can lead the Native
to a dietetically groaning table but you cannot make him lap up the
vitamins, phosphates, calories, and other nutritive abstractions.

When it comes to the step between Column A and Column B, between what is scientifically advisable and its practical application,
much wider and more comprehensive issues are involved. Here again,
the anthropologist obviously comes in. For it is not impossible to
change the Native economy, albeit slightly and gradually. Nor is it
impossible after prolonged study to suggest a scheme for the marketing of food produce. Some tribes who previously were only pastoral
have now been made to adopt agriculture—to mention only one, the
Hehe of Tanganyika Territory. Meat marketing has been extensively
developed among tribes who were formerly predominantly vegetarian,
such as the Chagga on the Kilimanjaro. Thus in Column B, biological
and medical research has to be supplemented by anthropological field
work, particularly in contact areas such as mine compounds, labor
camps, schools, locations, slum yards, townships, and in tribal reserves
with new economic trends in food production.

Here in order to assess the mechanisms of change and in order to
make fruitful suggestions for a progressive development of new
sources of food and of new habits of nutrition, the study of indigenous
and traditional feeding habits and commissariat is necessary. This belongs to Column C. Apart from the general study of the main systems
of food supply, we would have to investigate the substance of the
standard Native diet, the technique of its preparation, the way in

3. *Vide* E. B. Worthington, "On the Food and Nutrition of African Natives," *Africa,*
IX (1936), 153–154.

SYNOPTIC CHART FOR
PROBLEMS OF NATIVE DIET IN THEIR ECONOMIC SETTING

A	B	C
WHITE INFLUENCES, INTERESTS, AND INTENTIONS	PROCESSES OF CULTURE CONTACT AND CHANGE	SURVIVING FORMS OF TRADITION
1. Policy of control: a) administrative regulations (minimum rations, hygienic control of food supply); b) medical; c) economic (work of the agricultural department); d) educational; e) missions and beer (cf. B2, C2, B3, C3); puritanic taboos on pleasure and conviviality in food.	1. Actual efficiency of dietetic rules imposed. The relation of medical, educational, and economic agencies in the final results as observed in the contact areas. Introduction of new food crops. The influence of economic crops on food supply in reserves. Use of money for food. Food preferences and marketing. Illicit liquor (see below, 2).	1. The indigenous system of food supply. Production of food in agriculture, cattle breeding, fishing, hunting. (The food value of this produce; its chances of rational utilization and economic development.) Food supply from abroad by Native system of marketing and exchange. Periods of plenty and scarcity—seasonal and occasional.
2. Policy and practice of European enterprise—mines, plantations, farms. Payment in cash and rations (quota of income for payment of labor should be related to B1 and C4). Economic considerations (expense of better food in relation to increase in efficiency and improvement in health).	2. The supply and use of rations served to indigenous labor in mine compounds, etc. Appreciation and complaints. Use of money to supplement rations. Illicit liquor traffic and its nutritive, economic, and social implications.	2. The traditional standards of Native diet. Techniques of preserving and preparing. Diet and meals as a system of domestic routine. Tastes; value; social and religious aspects of food. Beer and other stimulants in private and tribal life.
3. Scientific research and planning. Physiological and medical research (work in Kenya and other East African colonies; laboratory research in South Africa, etc.). Translation of dietetic theory into practical rules and devices (work in Congo, on mines on Rand).	3. Working of scientific prescriptions in diet in contact areas. The relation of nutritive rules to the wider context of commensalism, social significance of meals and of food. The effect of puritanic taboos, especially on liquor in contact areas.	3. Effect of new tastes and habits on traditional nutritive systems. *This data for a Column E.*
4. Scientific assessment of the demands made by industrial labor on the organism of the African.	4. Adaptation of workers to European labor. Conditions (social, mental, and physiological) as re-	4. Influence of male exodus on indigenous food production and consumption.

A	B	C
WHITE INFLUENCES, INTERESTS, AND INTENTIONS	PROCESSES OF CULTURE CONTACT AND CHANGE	SURVIVING FORMS OF TRADITION
(Application of devices and methods of industrial psychology to African labor.)	gards food in which the "raw" Native comes to work. Change in health, efficiency, tastes during period of adaptation. The Belgian "labor farming" experiment.	(Use of money earned for agricultural improvements; purchase of land, implements. *This data for a Column E.*)

which it is consumed, and last but not least, things such as Native beer in the social structure and ceremonial life of the tribe; or cattle in their ritual and religious aspects.[4] Here we would have the necessary correlation between conservative trends, due not to any "inherent Native conservatism" but to the fact that the taking of food is an integral part of complex institutions and cannot therefore be treated as an independent variable; it must be related to new modes of feeding, of the production of food, and of its cultural utilization in the widest sense. If we realize how strong are food prejudices in Europe, and how they divide one nation from another, and how hard it is to overcome them, we need not speak contemptuously about African food conservatism. The English are quite as supercilious about the consumption of frogs and snails south of the Channel as the French are about the simplicity and crudeness in taste of the nation which has a hundred religions but only one sauce. The caste system of India, and rank divisions throughout the world, are associated with food and table manners. The same state of affairs is naturally to be found in Africa, and has to be treated scientifically, that is, with a certain amount of sympathy as well as intelligence.

Most of what has emerged from the previous discussion is already embodied in the synoptic scheme. The reader who submits it to a careful scrutiny will realize that it has been constructed on the same plan

4. The important monograph of Dr. A. I. Richards and Dr. E. M. Widdowson in this field show that it would be futile for the biochemist to organize and project his data without taking into account such anthropological evidence as the economics of food producing; the organization of consumption and preparation of food; the uneven social interest and cultural importance of certain foodstuffs, some of which, like millet or Kaffir corn, may be important because they are used on ceremonial occasions; while others, like meat and milk, enter into religion, distinctions as to sex, age, and rank. *Vide* "A Dietary Study in North-Eastern Rhodesia," *Africa*, IX (1936).

as the previous chart on African Warfare. Column D, incorporating the results of historical reconstruction, has been omitted for reasons of simplicity. We could place there under 1 "The indigenous systems of tribal economy as a self-sufficient and limited source of food supply." We could add there, besides the ordinary social organization of an economic character, "Slavery as a factor in food production." The last item is either completely extinct or else plays a subservient role; and since the supply of new slave labor is no longer available, it is irrelevant for future planning. "External sources of food through war and loot" are also a thing of the past. "Food supply from abroad by Native systems of marketing and exchange" and "Periods of plenty and scarcity, occasional and seasonal" would correspond to similar entries in Column C. But in olden days the facts to be found under these entries would unquestionably have a different form and significance. Again, this would have a great theoretical interest but hardly any practical relevancy for problems of guidance in culture change.

We could also investigate in Column D "The standard of diet in the olden days"; "the social and economic implications of this"; "the role of the chief or headman as host in tribal festivities"; "the consumption of food in tribal gatherings and beer drinks." The comparison of this column with C would be interesting for the anthropologist, in that it would reveal in the case of each particular area and tribe all those elements which have contributed to a change in food habits and supply of food. It would also be of value to see how far in the various regions of Africa the Native has gained economically as regards the very fundamentals of wealth—that is, in the quantity and quality of his diet. That an improvement in this respect is not universal seems to me a foregone conclusion. In many parts of South Africa there obtains a progressive pauperization of the Native community, as will be appreciated by anyone who reads for instance the Report of the last Native Economic Commission.[5] A shortage of lands, the deterioration and erosion of pastures, the considerable drain on male labor have inevitably impoverished the household on the reserves. Of an important section of the indigenous population, Dr. Hunter tells us "that the 'farm native' has lost economically by contact with Europeans. Working very much harder than he did under tribal conditions, he has no more nourishing and varied a diet than the rawest Pondo of the reserves." [6] The urbanized Native, for his part, is seldom able to balance his budget satisfactorily, and it is the nutrition of his womenfolk and children that suffers most severely. It would be difficult, however, to

5. Report of the Native Economic Commission, 1930–32, par. 69.
6. Hunter, *Reaction to Conquest*, p. 517.

compare in detail the historical past with the present, for here again we can provide objective data for the assessment of welfare conditions under the present regime, but lack the essential scientific observations of pre-European tribal conditions. Whenever we come to a really important problem of change, reconstructed history is lacking in the very essence of the subject matter.

We can see in our synoptic chart, however, that what is really necessary for a scientific statement of present-day conditions is the knowledge of the strongholds of Native tradition in food customs. Indeed, the very principle on which our table is built demands the study of each question under three headings. Take for instance 1 in Column C. These statements refer to the indigenous food supply in a given tribe, which obviously must be studied at first in its economic setting as defined by our successive entries. If we were to apply them to the only tribe where such an investigation has been systematically carried out by Dr. A. Richards—the Bemba of Northern Rhodesia [7]— we should find that the most important indigenous agricultural product is millet. As an economic crop, however, this is subject to pests such as locusts and to the vicissitudes of the climate, and the harvest may in dry years be insufficient. Since, moreover, this depends on the male labor in the community, the absence of men at work in the mines has been detrimental to Native agriculture. The Agricultural Department of the Colony has made a well-planned attempt at introducing new food crops, notably kassava. These efforts of the Department we could list under Column B. The assessment of this item, however, as a piece of planned improvement has to be referred to both Columns A and C.

As regards A, we should find, in submitting this improvement to physiological and medical research (A3), that kassava is deficient in fat as compared with millet. In the Bemba area where, owing to the tsetse fly, the Natives are unable to rear cattle and have not the necessary intake of fat in milk or meat,[8] a complete change to kassava diet might turn out to be physiologically pernicious. Thus we see that a planned change, which would be excellent from the economic point of view, might be entirely undesirable medically. Fortunately, the correlation between Columns B and C tells us that the danger is not imminent. The Bemba prefers, through long traditional molding, his

7. *Vide* Dr. Richards, *Hunger and Work in a Savage Tribe* (1932), and *Land, Labour and Diet in Northern Rhodesia* (1939).
Dr. Richards was also a member of the Diet Committee of the International Institute of African Languages and Cultures, which was a group of anthropologists, medical and nutritional experts set up in 1935 to make a study of nutrition among African tribes.
8. Richards, "A Dietary Study in North-Eastern Rhodesia," *Africa*, IX (1936), 195.

heavy millet porridge, and for social and even religious reasons he is in need of his traditional beer which is brewed from millet.[9]

What then would be the practical conclusions to be drawn from such a correlated study under the three headings? Obviously that it is not desirable to revolutionize Native agriculture completely, even were it possible to do so, for this would disorganize a great many of the indigenous institutions, ceremonial, domestic, and economic. Furthermore, any deliberate policy designed to bring about change would have to recognize another important conclusion which has emerged from our analysis: the fact that in such a delicate matter as diet a very careful and detailed correlation between the work of the various European agencies must be considered.

Returning to our table, the next point which we meet in the column of "Culture Change" is the introduction of economic crops for export. In Tanganyika, the agricultural department is attempting carefully and effectively to develop Native production of coffee and other economic products. The settlers on the other hand are pressing toward legislative limitation of such activities, citing the example of Kenya, where in some districts the Natives are forbidden to grow coffee. They give all sorts of reasons and publish them in more or less technical pleas for such legislation. Thus at first it is often alleged that the cultivation of coffee and tea by the Natives, side by side with Europeans, is dangerous for the European crops, since the Natives are unable to carry out a systematic prophylaxis against insect pests and other diseases of the plants.[10] Only a careful investigation through intensive and impartial field work in culture change (that is, the study of how far Natives can follow the advice of the agricultural demonstrator, and whether they can carry out plant hygiene as carefully as the White settler) can give a decisive answer to such questions. For it is important to open up for the Africans a new avenue of economic development. They need money for taxes and for trade goods. It is therefore clear that any all-round progress must be built on the foundations of a gradually increasing wealth.

9. *Idem*, p. 173.

In the subject of nutrition we would have also to consider the puritanic encroachments of Europeans, notably the influence of missions, which often affect Native conviviality, practices in food, and, above all, Native drinks. Missions and beer have to be listed under A1. One of the important questions for the anthropologist to discuss in conjunction with missionaries is whether it is wise to impose very rigid standards on African Christians in what might be called matters affecting *joie de vivre*. Apart from being one of the main hindrances to the success of evangelizing, extreme puritanism has made Christianity a wedge driven through every African tribe. See also Dr. Hunter's *Reaction to Conquest*, pp. 351, 355, for similar data.

10. Mair, *Native Policies in Africa*, p. 91.

At the same time it would be equally important that the educational and agricultural agencies should keep alive in the Native the necessity of not neglecting his own household crops for domestic consumption. His home farm is still the mainstay of his livelihood. Again, the marketing of Native produce for export is not perhaps as fully organized as a well-capitalized European enterprise. It is much more directly affected by the fluctuations of the world economic markets, and if, in any region, the Natives relied exclusively on export crops, they might be faced with periodic onsets of famine. As far as I am aware, this danger is not yet imminent in any part of Africa. On the other hand, there are regions where the use of Native labor, not for indigenous production but for White enterprise, is affecting the tribal food supply to a considerable extent. This, as we know, is the case among the Bemba; it also occurs in most of the South African reserves in the Union and the Protectorates, and it influences certain East African tribes.[11] If we look under Nos. 2, 3, and 4 in our three columns, we see that while the food given directly to the African laborer may be, and on the whole is, an inadequate compensation for the greater strain to which he is submitted, yet it is the only price paid for the abstraction of a large quota of male labor from indigenous production. Study of an interesting article by Dr. Orenstein [12] will convince the anthropologist that a great deal of competent research has been devoted to the diet of mine Natives. The visitor to the mines controlled by Dr. Orenstein's organization is also impressed by the quality of the food, the cleanliness and care used in its preparation, and the great consideration given to the differential tastes and idiosyncrasies of each tribe. But when we look at the facts in a comprehensive way, as suggested by our synoptic table, especially under entries 3 and 4, one or two questions emerge.

The excellent feeding on the mines is given to the 300,000 people, but it is given at the expense of abstracting their labor from their tribal economy. The women and children who remain at home undoubtedly suffer, especially in communities where 60 or 70 per cent of the able-bodied men are permanently absent. From the point of view of a long-range policy, is this a sound adjustment? Obviously it would have to be clearly stated that such limited dietetic efforts do not and cannot raise the general level of health and efficiency in the tribe.

Such considerations have apparently led in the Belgian Congo to an interesting experiment: a radical and ambitious scheme for supply-

11. *Idem*, pp. 39, 58–59, 71, 93, 106.
12. A. J. Orenstein: "The Dietetics of Natives Employed on the Witwatersrand Gold Mines," *Africa*, IX (1936), 218 ff.

ing permanent labor to the mines.[13] Instead of drafting the men from the tribal areas, as occasion demands, by systems of recruiting, some mining enterprises in the Congo have organized permanent settlement in the mining area where the workers live in families and are cared for medically, educationally, and economically. The dietetic care begins before the birth of the child; pregnancy has to be reported, the woman is fed and looked after during gestation and the period of suckling; children from the fourth year of age are fed by the mines or at least receive additional food rations connected with their attendance at nurseries and schools. Whether this experiment would arouse the enthusiasm of the anthropologist is doubtful, though it has points on moral grounds. If we profess in our policies that the administrative and industrial enterprise, directed and controlled from Europe, introduces dietetic improvement in the interest of the Native community as a whole, the South African feeding of labor during the period of service does not answer the challenge. For the families of the absentee laborers not only remain outside the scope of the improved diet but actually suffer scarcity through the absence of the main food producers. And we must not forget here that at times well over 50 per cent are away from the tribal area. In addition, the men develop new ideas, new tastes and habits in food, which quite as often as not make them dissatisfied with their own diet and thus unable to settle at home. Is it not, as is naïvely admitted, an extra inducement to return to the mines? [14] This is satisfactory from the point of view of the mine owner. But is it not one of the many factors leading to the disorganizing of the Native economy and even to difficulties in African home life?

13. *Vide* G. Trolli, "L'Alimentation chez les travailleurs indigènes dans les exploitations commerciales, agricoles, industrielles et minières au Congo," *Africa*, IX (1936), 197–217.

14. *Vide* A. W. Hoernlé's Supplementary Note to Orenstein's "The Dietetics of Natives Employed on the Witwatersrand Gold Mines," p. 225.
The fieldworker describing a group of Natives fed directly by Whites under a planned nutritive policy would analyze the conditions under which the food is taken; the number of meals per day; actual conditions of meals, whether in haste or leisure, whether immediately after work or during work. He would not bother for the time being with documentary evidence as to what the Natives are said to do. He would study the amount of food given, the actual way in which it is prepared and consumed. He would also study Native preferences, and from statements of Natives try to ascertain their opinions about the nutritive policies of the mines; how far there are tribal differences in response. Also it would be essential to discover the amount of food purchased by Natives, illicit liquor consumed, traffic in legitimate rations, etc. Against this data of Column B, we should have to state in Column A explicit and avowed European policies.

Is there any positive suggestion to make? The payment in cash received by African labor on the mines and elsewhere ought to be regarded, on broad and sociological lines, as the compensation to the whole tribe for the labor taken away. If the money thus earned could be employed so that the nourishment of women and children in the reserves is provided for, this aim would be achieved. Thus our study of the question of whether wages paid to Native laborers constitute an adequate compensation for their absence from the reserves leads us to a scientifically framed problem. How far is the average maximum wage paid to the African adequate in the sociological sense of the word? Our chart suggests to us [by a comparison of B_1, the general food supply through total tribal income, with C_1, the indigenous food supply] the conclusion that what we are taking away in labor ought to be made good by an improvement in tribal economy. What may be called the nutritive efficiency of an African tribe or detribalized group is certainly a minimum of the economic requirements. If the integral influence of European enterprise lowers the nutritive efficiency of African groups, then we are exploiting the African in a manner which is beyond any moral or political argument. I can bring forward these considerations only as suggestions for further research; but it is just this sort of suggestion, this constructive framing of problems for future field work and analysis, which should form the very essence of a sociological theory of culture change, relevant both theoretically and as a humanistic, common-sense charter for practical policies.

As an instrument for research and for the correlation of results, our chart has been useful in several ways. When the construction of each column allows us to correlate the various factors and agencies, we see for instance that European policies are determined not by consistent tendencies or trends but by many conflicting interests. The missionary with his dislike of beer and of meat used heathen fashion; the administrator attempting to regulate rations and generally to look after Native welfare; the agricultural officer taking at times a limited economic view; and the medical man looking at food as a biological factor and as a prophylactic against disease—all of these can be assisted by the anthropologist, who attempts to introduce some order and consistency into the welter of their intentions. But it is, above all, in the general economic trends of European enterprise, of these intentions often directed from the Bourse or the City, that we would find the greatest inconsistencies. Among the various economic influences of Europe in Africa, it is especially in relation to the nutritive supply that we come up against the problem of adequate recompense, not only in the spoon feeding of labor actually employed but in raising the nutritive standard of the tribe as a whole.

Our table also shows clearly the irrelevance of zero point or Column D. It shows very well also the fallacy of presuming that the White in Africa is a "well-integrated part of the tribe." Whether he be a missionary whose influence is, in a way, disintegrating tribal unity, or the entrepreneur whose whole policy is determined by elements outside Africa, we have to register his general aims and the technique of his procedure in a separate column, and then only see how he acts in the Native community. In the synoptic table, I have made one or two entries in Column C which really belong to Column E, that is, to factors in a new integration. The nutritive tastes, interests, and appreciations in food are probably among the most vital factors in the rising standard of African expectations. The intelligent, educated Native will inevitably sooner or later chance on some such considerations as were presented above.

XI

AFRICAN LAND PROBLEMS

LAND is unique among human possessions as that gift of God or nature which affects and benefits and is available to the community as a whole. Human beings live on it, live by it, and sometimes for it. It is an object which in Africa determines fundamental policies and is the key to good and bad relations between Black and White. The problem of its control is one of the most vital aspects of change, yet it creates the paradox that while its alienation may be necessary, this may in turn prevent sound contact. The land question bristles with issues of the common measure: with those common interests, conflicts, or compromises connected with general title, labor, and exploitation of resources. In so far as European policy is guided solely by the concept of Africa as the White Man's Country, and envisages wide European settlement and alienation of Native lands, it is difficult to find a common factor except in such terms as the "dignity of labor" (usually unskilled) or "profit by example" (segregation). Yet a common factor which will involve a recognition of both Native and European interests can be found, as will be shown later.

Here, as in other aspects we have examined, we shall not be concerned with the historical argument as a harking back to an ideal status, to the use of land prior to European contact. On the contrary, we want the wide vision of future development under a Dual Mandate, and the main question can be reduced to one which is extremely simple and quantitative: whether there is or is not enough land? Hence it is primarily a technical problem.[1]

All my arguments are not directed against the use of history as long as historical documents exist. But when as anthropologists we approach a problem where our knowledge is *ex hypothesi* of paramount value and yet deliberately turn to that phase, the past, where this knowledge fails, in order to use it and misuse it for a full and correct knowledge of the present, we have reached an absurdity. The more so when it is recognized that the process of change needs its own techniques and is a special field.

It is true that at each stage in the past we have a historical record

---

1. *Vide* Malinowski, "Practical Anthropology" (*Africa*, Vol. VII [1929], p. 30) where as early as 1929 he stressed that "the whole problem remains a groping in the dark as long as we are not able to ascertain what the necessary minimum for the Natives can be." Ed.

of the paper programs of European intentions, as crystallized in documents, recorded in proceedings of deliberative bodies, or in histories such as those of Sir Harry Johnston and Lord Lugard. But the paper program is never the actuality of contact. We have only to look at the Transkei where the original purpose was the transformation of the Natives into moderately prosperous small farmers, working their land under a system of individual land tenure, yet as a body still in need of employment, to see that such policies are never realized; [2] or again, to consider Uganda where the original vision is at variance with the real *status quo* and has led and had to lead to results entirely unforeseen. Or take the history of the Union between 1913 and 1936 where plans and recommendations of commissions were drafted and scrapped.

At each stage of history there has existed the practical task of implementing such programs: the working out in reality; the surveying; the interference of the old and the new; and the real occasions of contact. The machinery of change should have been placed under the microscope of actual observation of concrete instances; and it is here in such field work that the anthropologist and the administrator might have been a useful pair of co-workers. The field work on change would have had to ascertain at each period not only what was the new constitution of land tenure, as decreed and decided upon by the administration; the nature of such drastic policies as the cleaning up of squatters, the demarcation of reserves, the measures of the Uganda Treaty of 1900; but also the practice of White officials in contact with the Natives in the carrying out of such programs. Were such field work available at the time, it would have been of the greatest theoretical interest and would have furnished us with valuable lessons for the future.

Unfortunately, even the official documents which we have, while they provide elaborate data on European intentions, are very vague about Native needs. Native conditions were, so to speak, treated as a *tabula rasa*, and policies in the beginning were framed without direct reference to them. Thus in South Africa, in the early empirical stage of its history, there was an abundance of land loosely occupied by Bushmen and Hottentots, and the first settlers took up large areas, relying on imported slaves for labor.[3] Efforts were made to segregate

2. *Vide* Raymond L. Buell, *The Native Problem in Africa*, I, 92, where it is pointed out that individual tenure in surveyed areas has not produced a better type of agriculture; that Natives who have titles still cling to communal conceptions of property; and that younger sons, who under the older system would have had land, are now forced out into the labor market.

3. For the whole of this chapter on African Land Problems, Malinowski had only penciled notes with the exception of the typescript dealing with land tenure among the

the Natives from the Whites from 1812 onward, but these proved abortive, since the desire for labor and trade made contact inevitable; and in 1828 the Cape admitted Natives for work and permitted them to hold land.[4] Later the Fingo were given reserves, but the Bantu tribes were driven back before the desire of the Whites for new land on the frontiers. The Boers became restive under a policy which henceforth was to be orientated toward assimilation; they formulated the principle: [5] "There shall be no equality between black and white either in Church or State"; and they began their Great Trek north.[6] However, as Dr. Mair has pointed out, "in practice the Cape policy has worked out in a manner not widely different from that of the Boer Republics. The practical disadvantages under which the Native population is placed are similar throughout the Union, though the legislative enactments affecting their position are less severe in the Cape than elsewhere." [7] In other words, while the Natives were to be regarded "as a part of ourselves with a common faith and common interests," [8] little attempt was made to examine and meet those interests, and when the government took over the Native territories of Griqualand and Bechuanaland, land was again alienated to the Whites. In Natal locations were set aside for the Natives, though sometimes with an eye to providing a reservoir of labor for Europeans near by; and in 1864 the Natal Native Trust was created to administer the lands.[9]

Even the attempts to introduce individual land tenure as a civilizing measure paid little or no attention to the type of agriculture practiced by the Natives and to its future development. They were, moreover, motivated frequently by a desire to force onto the labor market those Natives who could not afford lots, or who would have to obtain money for surveying fees and the upkeep of the land. Out of this came the Glen Grey Acts of 1894 for the Transkei, where individual tenure was established and a tax of ten shillings was to be imposed on able-bodied men who were not working. Supporting the measure before the Legislative Assembly, Cecil Rhodes asserted: "You will remove them [the

Baganda and the Pondo. In some cases the notes were sufficiently full to be used as they stood, apart from a rearrangement of paragraphs and the addition of footnotes. But for the section dealing with the history of European settlement there were only headings and references to Buell's book; and I have therefore filled in the details for the sake of continuity and completeness. Ed.

4. Sheila Van Der Horst, *Native Labour in South Africa*, p. 13. *Vide* also Mair, *Native Policies in Africa*, p. 22.
5. Art. 9 of the Transvaal Grondwet (Constitution).
6. Mair, *op. cit.*
7. *Ibid.*
8. Van Der Horst, *op. cit.*, p. 17, quoting Sir George Grey.
9. Buell, *op. cit.*, p. 72.

Natives] from that life of sloth and laziness, you will teach them the dignity of labour, and make them contribute to the prosperity of the State, and make them give some return for our wise and good government." However the tax was repealed in 1905.[10]

Until 1913 Natives had been able to purchase land outside reserves, but with the passing of the Lands Act they were henceforth forbidden to do this; in other words, the policy of segregation was incorporated into the legislation. This meant that for the time being the Natives had no rights to legal tenure in 92 per cent of the Union,[11] though more land was to be granted for reserves, and Natives working on farms could remain where they were, and in the Transkei they could not be evicted. Soon afterward, the Beaumont Commission recommended areas for reserves, but these were cut down everywhere except in the Cape, and its decisions were not acted upon until 1927.[12]

The results of such a policy in its disregard in practice of Native needs have become evident in various reports, in the Native Economic Commission (1930–32), and even more recently in a White Paper of 1936: "Speaking generally, it is notorious that the existing native locations and reserves are congested, denuded, over-stocked, eroded, and for the most part, in a deplorable condition." [13] A similar disregard of Native interests has also been shown in legislation relating to the imposition of taxes (frequently with the avowed aim of forcing Natives onto the labor market); in the discriminative acts limiting wages, occupations, and attaching criminal sanctions to Native contracts; in the restrictions on freedom of movement as embodied in the pass laws; and in regulations for Native squatters. All these reveal a state of affairs in which the land hunger of the Whites, and their need for a cheap unskilled labor which will not compete with European employment have been allowed to override Native interests.[14]

However, in outlining thus briefly the history of European policy, it must be remembered that the criticism leveled against it is based on its results, as we know them at the present day. Hence such legislation represents possibilities out of which there might have been a dif-

10. Van Der Horst, *op. cit.*, p. 149.
11. Buell, *op. cit.*, p. 82.
12. *Idem*, p. 84.
13. Quoted by Van Der Horst, *op. cit.*, p. 304.
14. For a detailed account of such legislation the reader is referred to Buell, *op. cit.*, Vol. I; Mair, *op. cit.*; and Van Der Horst, *op. cit.* The last is the most recent (1942) and while it contains little detailed criticism of policy and few suggestions for the future, its description in detail of legislation presents an indictment of certain aspects of the economic system in South Africa.

The text of the rest of this section is almost directly reproduced from Malinowski's notes. Ed.

ferent development; it bears witness to opportunities missed and misused. But the conditions under which it was inaugurated are no longer available, and their reconstruction is a knowledge which cannot be applied now. We can, however, learn something from European administration, if only from what it failed to achieve, from the problems it has created, and from Native grievances at present. It teaches that Native interests cannot be regarded as either nonexistent or indefinitely pliable; that Native progress requires the reservation for them of land and good land at that. All these conclusions provide us with a moral lesson, but it is still wisdom after the event. Had our tripartite scheme for the study of culture contact been applied during the earlier periods, it would have provided invaluable material for the framing of such policies as the Glen Grey Acts, the Lands Act of 1913, and so on. But considering that land tenure is one of the key problems, it is extraordinary how little discussion there is of it in such books as those by Junod, Smith, Dale, Rattray, Dudley Kidd, and Torday. Moreover from these early accounts of African land tenure, all change has been carefully cleaned off the picture; all traces of European influences have been expunged. While from the point of view of reconstruction this is legitimate, the sociologist, as the chronicler of contemporary history in one of its most significant phases, cannot shut his eyes to what is going on now and conjure figments up from nowhere.

We must therefore postulate the need for a study which will show:

A. Plans (intentions and interests); legal acts; economic reforms, and the manner in which these are translated into effective action all along the line: i.e., in the districts, in the agricultural schools, and right among the Native pastures and fields.

B. The interaction of such plans and acts with Native response, opposition, acceptance and readjustment.

C. The tribal conditions, which in most cases still survive bodily in large areas, and which endure for a long time, with some modifications through and within change, and on which action as under A has to be exercised.[15]

D. The reconstruction of the old system of land tenure.[16]

E. The new tendencies, the movements which crystallize in response to a strong sense of Native grievances over lack of land, over discrimination in industry and on the farms.

Here, as previously, the line of demarcation between these columns

15. Here also we must study those memories of the old time which survive; the legal and religious values which hold sway in attitudes to land; the authority of the chief, of the council, and of the clan in regard to land.

16. Column D was not included in the penciled notes but occurs on a chart drawn up by Malinowski and obviously has its place here. Ed.

is clearly defined. A and B must be kept and considered apart, in so far as there is a distinction between policy and its execution. White ideas and interests, greeds and good intentions, must be measured up against the reality of present conditions. B and C must also remain separate. In B we have the land as owned and used by the Natives under individual tenure; in C we have land as used by the Natives through their old system. C is often not recognized by A; but on the whole the less discrepancy there is between Columns B and C, the less likelihood there is of friction. Under an ideal Indirect Rule, the policy of A, in so far as it bears on Native interests, should have been instructed by C. Likewise C and D we have distinguished as existing institutions and living history on the one hand and as the reconstructed past on the other.

The White Man's Country

The "White Man's Country," as a territorial policy in Africa, has meant that the country is to be reserved primarily for the development of European settlement. Hence in our analysis of the land problem it figures as one of the most important factors in our Column A of European interests and plans, and while its implementation has varied in different parts of Africa, it has involved in the past the successive alienation of the best lands of Europeans and the drafting (in all but name) of Native labor for their exploitation.

Before discussing it, however, we may glance for a moment at the situation in parts of the French and Belgian colonies where the Concessions Policy has had similar effects in so far as Native interests are concerned,[17] namely, the dispossession of Natives of their lands. For instance, in French Equatorial Africa the government reserved to itself the right to grant large areas to companies; and although parts were to be put aside for the Natives, nothing was done to delimit these except for an *arrêté* of 1903 which proposed granting the Natives 10 per cent of the conceded territory and 6 per cent of the total production of rubber. In order to insure an adequate labor supply, a tax was imposed on the Natives, and the net result of the concession regime was that "it took away the land from the natives, and obliged them to

---

17. A comparable policy was followed by the British Government in Northern Nigeria from 1886 to 1900, during which period a charter was held by the Royal Niger Company, granting it mining rights and administrative powers. *Vide* Buell, *op. cit.*, p. 682. In the Gold Coast concessions were also granted, but by 1925 they represented only 1 per cent of the total area of the colony. *Vide* Mair, *op. cit.*, p. 161.

In Malinowski's manuscripts there were brief notes on French and Belgian Africa, and I have therefore added some details in order to complete this section. Ed.

collect rubber for the companies." [18] Appalling atrocities occurred and were brought to public notice.[19] After 1910 the concession areas were reduced and some of the companies were merged into the Compagnie Forestière Sangha-Oubanghi, which had a monopoly over rubber. Since 1923 greater efforts have been made to safeguard the recruiting of Natives and the conditions under which they work; nevertheless the construction of the railway by the Batignolles Company led to the conscription of Natives for labor, although the number guaranteed by the government has been reduced from time to time.[20]

In French West Africa fewer concessions have been granted, except in the Ivory Coast; the Native production has been encouraged. Here too, however, the government assisted private enterprise in the recruiting of labor, and as late as 1923 was reported as furnishing a set number of men for the Compagnie des Cultures Tropicales en Afrique.[21] In both colonies adult male Natives are obliged to give service to the government for ten or fifteen days under the prestation system; and under another semimilitary organization, the *Smotig*, those not actually required for service with the troops are put to work on operations of public importance.[22]

In the Belgian Congo, there was a period during the Leopoldian regime when large concessions were granted, and atrocities committed against the Natives. Since then, there have been restrictions on European enterprise and some attention has been paid to Native interests. Nevertheless concessions were still granted to various companies for the construction of railways and oil mills, and for the exploitation of wild products and mines. On paper Native rights were to be respected, but no surveys were made, and often the rights of Native villages in regard to hunting, fishing, and collecting of wild fruits were ignored.[23] While there is not the land scarcity that constitutes an urgent problem in other parts of Africa, there is a tendency for the best lands to pass into the hands of the concessionaires. As far as trade is concerned, the Natives living in the Huileries Concession must sell their produce to the company at rates which are below market price.[24]

On the other hand, since 1926 labor regulations in the Belgian Congo seem to be more liberal and effective than those obtaining in the

18. Buell, *op. cit.*, II, 234–235.
19. *Idem*, pp. 233, 236 ff.
20. Mair, *op. cit.*, p. 205.
21. Buell, *op. cit.*, p. 27.
22. Mair, *op. cit.*, p. 199.
23. *Idem*, pp. 221, 226.
24. *Idem*, p. 229.

majority of European dependencies in Africa.[25] Some attention has been paid the future development of Native agriculture, but the policy has been hampered by the large amount of recruiting, in spite of checks; and secondly by the adoption of a system which compels the Natives to grow such crops as manioc, rice, and cotton. While the fostering of Native production is obviously a step in the right direction, it appears in practice that Native interests have not always met with full consideration. Natives have not always received adequate remuneration for their efforts, and the administration has shown a lack of foresight in forcing the system on tribes which previously had no agriculture.[26] Dr. Mair in this connection makes a point which has been emphasized again and again throughout this book: "This is a striking example of a scheme which has failed through ignorance of the essential data of the problem—in this case the nature of the economic organization and standards of value with which the administration has to deal." [27] In other words, while the desire to exploit African natural resources on the one hand and the policy of maintaining a Native economy on the other provide us with a common factor of interest between the administration and the Natives in the development of Native agriculture, the implementation of that policy, as summarized in our Column B, has created conflict and resistance because it has not taken into account all the factors which we have listed in our Column C—native values and institutions.[28]

It is in some of the dependencies of East and South Africa that the ideal of the White Man's Country has entered as a most important factor in the annexations of land. North of the Union in certain tropical areas where the elevation is over 4,000 feet, regions are believed to be especially suitable for White settlement. Thus the principles determining the selection of lands have not been respect for Native rights but rather good climate, fertile soil, and cheap Native labor; the amenities of sport, outdoor life, and an exotic setting; an abundant and pliant domestic service or, in other words, a really comfortable house.[29] Obviously such a policy drives the Natives off the best

25. Some discussion of the measures taken to safeguard Native labor has already occurred in this book in the chapter on "Problems of Native Diet in Their Economic Setting."

26. Mair, *op. cit.*, p. 238.

27. *Idem*, p. 239.

28. The remainder of this section dealing with the White Man's Country in the British areas is taken *in toto* from Malinowski's penciled notes; only their order has been changed where it seemed necessary. Ed.

29. An example of this policy is to be found in the Morris Carter Commission of 1933 which defined the limits of the 16,700 square miles in Kenya which had been

lands and involves the creation of reserves. Nevertheless, such a plan for complete segregation is never carried through completely because White farmers require assistance and hence permit the presence of Native squatters; and secondly, because labor is required for industry and domestic service.

The effect on the reserves of draining off a large number of the male Natives as labor for the mines has already been discussed under nutrition. Here we can deal briefly with the plight of Natives living on farms in South Africa.[30] Obviously their presence precludes the possibility of any real segregation; at the same time White settlers cannot be regarded as an integral part of the tribe, for the very charter of their presence is based on the principle of a "White Man's Country" but "Black Man's Labor." The existence of these White farmers determines the lot of the Natives squatting on their land, and the Whites pass on to the Natives their economic stresses. From the chart on p. 124, we can see at a glance that the hard and strenuous conditions of Native labor cannot be appreciated without a study on the one hand of the corresponding entry in Column A: difficult economic conditions (as brought out in the report on the Poor Whites), with little leeway for increased expenditures; the need for strict discipline and means of coercion;[31] and, on the other, a reference to Column C: the overcrowding on reserves, the dislike of the reserve Native for the detribalized Native, and the fear of sorcery engendered by this attitude.

All this leads us to the question: under what conditions is farming in South Africa a pursuit leading to the mutual prosperity and well-being of Native and White? The answer to this need not involve any more metaphysical problem than the balancing of budgets of both Native laborer and farmer. Under the present conditions of the world market, the European farmer cannot make two ends meet and he requires a subsidy. The development of agriculture is largely met from revenue from gold mining, since the soil is not sufficiently fertile to compete against such countries as Argentina. Hence cheap labor becomes the only asset. This implies the curtailing of Native liberties, the taboo on trade-unions, combinations, and even social contacts; and

made available for European settlement by the White Paper of 1923. It should be noted, however, that Native interests with regard to land have been largely respected in Tanganyika, Nyasaland, Nigeria, and in other British dependencies of the West Coast.

30. Malinowski's notes on Native squatters are very few, but since they include the main points necessary for this section I have not amplified them. The reader, however, is referred to Buell, Mair, Van Der Horst, and Hunter for the details which substantiate his argument. Ed.

31. Dr. Hunter states in her *Reaction to Conquest* that membership in a trade-union is forbidden on practically all farms (see p. 508).

an attitude of repression toward Native churches and education.[32] What we therefore need, as a basis for the formulation of policy, is a specific anthropology of "Farmers in Contact"; for their presence determines the lot of many Natives; and in so far as a development of agriculture is envisaged, this is really the crux of the problem of White and Black Africa in the future.

When we turn to the appropriations made for Native reserves, we find that generally the best lands have been given to the Whites; and that even when good ones were made available, as to the Fingo in the early days,[33] they are no longer the best because of erosion and over-crowding. Elsewhere conditions on reserves have been such that owing to density of population, poverty, and heavy taxation, Natives have been unable to support themselves and have had to indenture for a period of time.[34]

Even when an attempt is made to improve such conditions by fostering Native peasant production, the Whites are likely to oppose it wherever it is likely to compete with their own interests.[35] Hence,

32. Dr. Hunter in *Reaction to Conquest* has dealt very fully with conditions of the Bantu on European farms, *vide* pp. 505 ff. She analyzes the inadequacy of wages (pp. 515–517); points out the restrictions on the grazing of cattle as a constant source of friction (p. 511); the bitterness over poverty, restrictions on visiting, and the performance of rituals on many farms (p. 507). Many of the farmers oppose education (p. 526); while "the performance of customary ritual killings is made difficult or impossible, membership in any church, except one controlled by Europeans, is forbidden on a number of farms, and membership in a trade-union on practically all" (p. 508).

For a further discussion of conditions of Native squatters, see Mair, *op. cit.*, pp. 32–35; Buell, *op. cit.*, I, 79–82; and Van Der Horst, *op. cit.*, pp. 282 ff.

33. The Fingo were in a more favorable position than other Natives and were able to grow sufficient for purposes of trade. *Vide* Van Der Horst, *op. cit.*, p. 27.

34. As early as 1903 there were reports that the reserves were insufficient to support the Natives (*vide* Mair, *op. cit.*, p. 27); while the Native Economic Commission in 1930–32 reported that "We have now throughout the Reserves a state of affairs in which, with few exceptions, the carrying capacity of the soil for both human beings and animals is definitely on the downgrade; a state of affairs, which unless soon remedied, will within one or at the outside two decades create in the Union an appalling problem of Native poverty." Quoted in Van Der Horst's *Native Labour in South Africa*, p. 304, n. 1.

35. For example, in Nyasaland where cotton and tobacco are largely in Native hands, the Nyasaland Planters' Association in 1926 protested against the effect of this on the labor market and declared it was to the detriment of the future of the European agricultural industry (Buell, *op. cit.*, I, 253). In Tanganyika, as a result of the agitation of European coffee growers, the government has withdrawn its encouragement of Native production since 1925 (Buell, *op. cit.*, pp. 475, 494). In Uganda, where the Natives have been successful in cotton growing, "the planters feel that Native agriculture is incompatible with European interests" (Buell, *op. cit.*, p. 629). Finally, in Kenya the Natives have been able to export some maize and cotton but they are forbidden to grow coffee (Buell, *op. cit.*, pp. 392–393). Ed.

Similar problems are also likely to arise in the Union wherever Native production is likely to compete with European interests. Already a Marketing Act of 1937 exercises

while the ideal of the White Man's Country necessarily points to segregation, other factors such as the desire for labor, the poor lands given to the Natives, and the fear of competition militate against such a policy. Finally, it is to be remembered that the missionaries carry on a program that breaks into this tribal life, makes it insecure and sometimes inadequate, creates new wants which can in part only be satisfied by acquiring European articles or adopting European institutions. Hence tribal reserves are ceasing to be tribal. In the long run a new class of Native is being created, at present small in number but inevitably increasing—the class of the Europeanized, civilized Native—for whom missionary and medical departments work, who is neither White nor yet the Native of the old tribal reserves.

Let us glance at our chart which shows the essentials of the segregation system. First and foremost we see that the system works as it does, with its effectiveness and maladjustments, because the three phases function side by side, each controlled by its own specific determinism. The tribal habits (C_1, C_2, and C_4) persisting as they do, largely because the economic scope of the Natives is cramped by squeezing them into reserves, are a handicap to economic development. They are one of the obstacles to full economic use (in the European sense) of the limited soil of the reserves. The strong economic solidarity of kindred works against individual enterprise, since a wealthy man has to share (C_2). Again, a plough agriculture implies more land, but there is only a small acreage for subsistence crops. Finally, the sentiment of the Native toward cattle, which is uneconomic and inelastic, makes for the deterioration of the soil (C_1). In all this, the action of European forces in restricting the portion of African soil to be set aside for African uses works as a conservative force, or at least as an opposing one, preventing any fuller use being made of the new, more efficient methods which are advocated and taught.

But these conditions, adverse to Native economic development, make for a large and also for an elastic supply of cheap labor, a factor indispensable to European policy under the "White Man's Country" system. Since the Natives must have subsistence, and have no means of obtaining ready cash, even tax money has to be earned by White employment. During a period when agricultural or even mining products fall in prices, the reserves make also for elasticity in supply, while the demand is allowed to remain as rigid as White interests require.

much control in favor of Europeans, and in 1938 the Secretary of the Livestock and Meat Industries Control Board affirmed that the competition of livestock of the Natives was a serious one for the White agriculturist. *Vide* Van Der Horst, *op. cit.*, pp. 310–311. Ed.

CHART DEFINING POLICY OF SEGREGATION AND RESERVES

A	B	C
WHITE INFLUENCES, INTERESTS, AND INTENTIONS	PROCESSES OF CULTURE CONTACT AND CHANGE	TRIBAL CONDITIONS ON RESERVES
1. "White Man's Country": general principles: large blocks of land marked off from tribal areas and kept clean of squatters and African *enclaves;* but well supplied with cheap Native labor and Native domestic staff. The soil to be economically good and opportunities for sport, especially hunting, to be present. Usually large tracts unused. Communications usually good.	1. "Segregation" in phrase; in reality, mutual dependence intrinsic in European situation (labor); as regards Africans, often artificially enforced by taxing, recruiting under pressure, and above all, inadequacy of opportunities in reserves. Thus though real segregation, as independence of both sections and full opportunities for both, would give full common measure of mutual satisfaction, "segregation" as planned and practiced is not favorable to the African.	1. The new tribal reserves, restricted in area, often lack the essentials needed for old African economy, such as variety of soil, room for occasional migration and expansion. Old economic activities, especially overstocking on a restricted area, often produce considerable deterioration of soil. Communications usually poor. From restrictions of his reserves, the African still glances across to tribal lands in A1—to ancestral graves.*
2. Education and general improvement in practical skills, given on principle by missionary, educational, agricultural, and medical services, are also useful, within limits, to settlers. Money economy, inherent to tax system and wage labor, is also needed if Native is to become customer of White commerce. Few attempts to guide use of money for improvement of reserves, etc.	2. Both education and money economy tend to raise standard of living and to Europeanize it. Yet even where traditional attitudes are shed, there is no scope for profitable investment (too little land, and usually none for sale; no economic enterprise with few exceptions). Thus money is often misused on unnecessary European objects. Yet under guidance and advice money could be used for improvement on reserves.	2. Persistence of indigenous standards of value and wealth (quantitative; appreciation of cattle; African conception of hospitality, generosity, and lavishness; Native tastes in food and drink). Political loyalties, kinship bonds antagonistic to personal accumulation of wealth.
3. A small class of educated, enterprising, independent Africans is formed. This class bids	3. Very limited provision for the educated class is made in special reserves. (Since it is likely that this	3. No room or opportunities for the educated class in reserves.

* Restrictions of land in (C1) primarily conduce to the African's need of selling his labor to (A1).

A	B	C
WHITE INFLUENCES, INTERESTS, AND INTENTIONS	PROCESSES OF CULTURE CONTACT AND CHANGE	TRIBAL CONDITIONS ON RESERVES

A	B	C
fair to be on increase. It is the result of those European agencies and influences (missionary and educational) that want the educated Native, and of those who need, hence use and train, him.	class will grow in numbers and influence, what disturbing influence will they have on the whole "segregation system"?)	
4. During slumps in European production (notably in mining but also in sisal, coffee, etc.) Native labor becomes superfluous.	4. Large numbers of unemployed males hang around mining camps, parasitic on employed workers. (The villages absorb another part, who usually remain drones.)	4. Tribal obligations of kinship, political paternalism, and neighborliness compel provision for the needy even if they through lack of use and skill are unable to take full part in tribal productive economy.

For, owing to the forces of traditional generosity, the strong vitality of kinship obligations and neighborly kindness, the unemployed can return to the reserves and share the pittance of tribal subsistence economy. In 1934 large numbers in search of employment on the Belt were kept by their kinsmen—of course at the expense of these and minus the money which would ordinarily have gone to the reserves. Thus the mining companies have an excellent system of unemployment insurance, the cost of which is borne by the Natives.

A very important issue, perhaps one of the most important, is listed in A3, B3, and C3. Royal Commissions, pro-Natives, and progressives complain of the vice of Native backwardness. Yet if we speed up development, we shall only increase the class formed by European influence (A3)—the educated, enterprising African. For this class there is no room either in C1 nor in A1; in the Native reserve or the European area. They will demand a territorial basis under a system of individual land tenure. If room is found for them, or if the system in C1 is translated into a European type, the whole balance of the policy of the White Man's Country will be upset. For it means that there will be no supply of cheap and elastic labor; no useful domestic material for the European who wants "the raw Native every time."

The ultimate decision as to policy will have to be made by the statesman. But the sociologist has to show that the implications of such a recommendation as that of the Native Economic Commission are highly revolutionary and even dangerous in so far as the future of the segregation system is concerned. For it means the improvement of reserves on a tribal basis rather than production by individual tenure and farms of a European character.

Thus our table which summarizes the argument enables us to analyze more clearly the policy of segregation as it actually works. B1 shows that the keynote is not real segregation but mutual dependence in a definite sphere of coöperation. C1 shows how the territorial restriction assists the persistence of the tribal system (C2). A2 introduces the side of European influence which works as a progressive factor necessary to A1 within limits, but threatening the whole system with ultimate undermining when it reaches the limit (B3).

Here also a few pertinent questions may be asked. Since the policy aims at promoting the interests of the White man and agricultural enterprise, we may ask if it is economically sound. Does it pay? Or is it a heavy burden on the British taxpayer and the Native? The White Man's Burden is that by cheap Native labor he can hope to make ends meet. But is this a genuine contribution to other aspects of colonial policy and to the second bidding of the Dual Mandate? If African resources can be exploited better in the long run by indigenous enterprise;[36] if one industry after another has to be subsidized [37] because it cannot compete with Central and South America, with coffee in Brazil, tea in India, meat in the Argentine, and so on, then the White Man's Country is a luxury rather than a productive asset. It becomes rather an extension of sporting sovereignty. Many of the settlers are in the receivers' hands; and a class of Poor Whites has been created. It may be that the White Man's Country is a luxury which can be afforded by the European side; but there is no necessity for the Natives to pay the price; and future generations of settlers may also have to pay it.

36. That such a system of Native peasant production can be successful is shown by the growing of ground nuts and cotton in French West Africa; of cotton in Uganda; of coffee and cotton in Tanganyika; of cotton and tobacco in Nyasaland; of cocoa in the Gold Coast; of cotton and ground nuts in Nigeria. Ed.

37. In South Africa the government has had to foster farming by granting land on easy terms with special credit facilities, assisted irrigation, drought relief, and subsidies on exports. *Vide* Van Der Horst, *op. cit.* J. M. Tinley in a recent book on *The Native Labor Problem of South Africa* also points out that the government has had to boost such industries as wine-growing, tobacco, sugar cane, wheat, dairy products, maize, and livestock by stabilizing prices, with the result that the consumers have to bear the brunt of the burden and production is sometimes expanded to areas not suitable for it (*vide* pp. 213–225). Ed.

Land Tenure Policies

The analysis of the reserve and segregation policy given in the chart on p. 124 will help us in dealing with legal title in its widest sense, from the rights assumed by the Crown down to the details of Native tenure and its administrative and legal handling. Obviously where there is no White settlement the problems are of much greater simplicity. Where there are White settlers, the ultimate solution may be one of reserves, and the question arises as to the type of policy to be followed in such areas.

Now on the face of it, land tenure seems to be a matter of legal title. Yet to consider title divorced from the context of the realities of use and life is intellectually preposterous. Unfortunately, in the hands of professional lawyers, accustomed to rigid formalism, shy of being sociologically or economically sidetracked, unversed in the anthropological game of "minimum definitions" and elastic concepts, the matter has been badly handled. It is as if one were to trust the bigoted and sectarian theologians of a narrow sect to decide on a common measure between the Wee Free Creed, totemism, ancestor worship, and Melanesian magic. They would be bound to blunder. That the lawyers have blundered can be seen in that many of their decisions have been reversed in practice; also in that many of their decisions have consisted in shirking decisions.

Before we outline this confusion and anarchy in the legal foundations of Natives' rights to live on their own soil, let us sketch out the positive approach. The main legal issue is: how to recognize, vest, and safeguard in perpetuity Native titles, so as to protect them from European rapacities. Titles have to be established which would protect them against European legal trickery and yet would not cut across the Native economic system. On the theoretical side, this involves finding a common factor between Native rights based on age-long use and occupation of land, and European legal systems. Can such a common factor be found? Emphatically, yes! There is first the European desire in certain territories to grant full security and undisturbed possession; secondly, the desire of the Natives to keep their lands and to work them without prejudicial interference from the Whites. Moreover we find that when it suits Europeans to leave a loophole to upset Native customary law, a principle of "natural justice and morals" is invoked. But this principle may also provide us with a common factor when it comes to upholding existing Native rights—for the *right to exist* on a level of elementary decency is indeed the fundamental principle of justice and equity.

One of the main difficulties up to now has been the inability of European lawyers to establish a definition of the legal right of the Natives in terms of anything except individual freehold.[38] The object has been to impose a European system, but here we may ask pertinently, what European system? Does this mean individual tenure under the Code Napoléon or under English Commons; or some type similar to absentee landlordism in Ireland, or the Polish peasant system under serfdom? To speak of European property as one "over which the owner has absolute rights and of which he can dispose without reference to others" is fantastically incorrect.[39] No such property exists even in European law, far less in European custom. Again, the practice of the Pondo Native going out to earn his living, while his family remains behind and works for him on his farm, may be paralleled in Europe by the emigrant who goes to America, while his farm is cared for by his wife and perhaps his relatives. Simply to say that the "individualistic" attitude is essentially good; that it is one of the characteristics of a new economic spirit, and a sound incentive to work—all this is a sociological misapprehension. Frequently the excessively "individualistic" attitude, as found among Natives, is not due to a conversion to European ways, but is an unhealthy sign of a midway existence on the no-man's level of cultural maladjustment.

Law, and law as it operates in a system of land tenure, must be taken for what it is: the sanctioned recognition of vital interests and essential rights of individuals, group, and integral community. It must be recognized that law grows out of social conditions, and cannot be imposed upon them except perhaps in revolutions, and that this in the long run usually proves abortive and falls into abeyance.[40] Thus we can establish the proposition that the duty of legal agencies of a colonial power, from the Privy Council to the Assistant Commissioner, in supervising a Native court or adjusting a village squabble, is to give force and formal recognition to existing rights and customs, unless those rise directly counter to European standards and susceptibilities.

When we come to tenure of land we are dealing with the legal

38. For instance, in 1918 in Southern Rhodesia the Judicial Committee of the Privy Council declared that the Natives to prove their rights would have to show that they belonged to the category of rights of private property. *Vide* Buell, *op. cit.*, I, 210. In Swaziland in 1926 the Privy Council also decreed that the title of the Native community took the form of usufructuary right, and that this was a mere qualification of a burden on final title of whoever is sovereign (*idem*, p. 200). Ed.

39. Statement quoted from Hunter, *Reaction to Conquest*, p. 130.

40. For Malinowski's theory of law, see his *Crime and Custom in Savage Society;* his review, "A New Instrument for the Interpretation of Law—Especially Primitive," *Yale Law Review*, XLI, No. 8 (1942), 1237–1254; and his Introduction to H. Ian Hogbin's *Law and Order in Polynesia*. Ed.

expression of the fundamental conditions of life. Here the anthropologist is on his own ground, for he has evolved his own methods for the collecting of evidence on land ownership and for its analysis.[41] The key to the problem lies in economic use. Land tenure is to be correlated with social organization; with occasional legal acts; with modes of disposal and inheritance; with type of utilization; and with sentimental values. Man everywhere surrounds his mother earth, the land which feeds him and the environment which gives him shelter and protection, with beliefs and ideas. He as a rule surrounds it with a mythical and historical tradition and defines his relation to land in more or less precise legal statements. At the same time he uses the land and appropriates, distributes and consumes the produce from it. It is, in my opinion, the correlation between the mythical and legal ideas on the one hand, and the economic activities on the other, which forms the substance of land tenure.[42]

All African tribes or tribelets, from the seminomadic Bushmen to the Baganda and the Chagga, have the right to reside in safety and in peace; the right to exploit their traditional plots or territory for a minimum subsistence according to standards which for them are indispensable. They have the right to enjoy certain amenities which to them make life worth living; the right to arrange for marketing, visiting, and communal gatherings; the right to cultivate and practice sacred ceremonies in sacred spots and to tend the graves of the ancestors. A system of Native land tenure, a codification of uses to which land is put, and of the rights of individuals and of groups, does exist. Here there can be no question of the fundamental principle involved: the right to possession in security and protection for the purpose of beneficial cultivation. Such rights must be recognized and firmly established. Unfortunate though it is, it may be necessary to limit some of these, but the Natives must be granted a substantial margin for subsistence.

Law then becomes here the formal recognition and sanctioning by European power with all its abilities to formulate, enact, and defend. If rights must be curtailed in some directions, the process can only be equitable if there are compensations. Here there is no question of returning to the original *status quo*. The very fact that the Europeans

---

41. For my own contributions on this problem, see *Coral Gardens and Their Magic* (1935). Similar methods and analysis are also utilized by Dr. R. Firth in his *Polynesian Economy;* by Dr. Richards in *Land, Labour and Diet in Northern Rhodesia;* and Dr. Mair in *An African People in the Twentieth Century.*

42. The passage beginning "Man everywhere" is from Malinowski's Introduction to Hogbin's *Law and Order in Polynesia,* p. xliii. He also gives a similar definition of land tenure in *Coral Gardens,* I, 319. Ed.

came, and that they control African soil and its production, even
though indirectly in some cases, is a complete annulment of any "original" rights or titles. What we shall need is a study of conditions as
they are now: in terms of present European policies which are being
executed; in terms of Native systems of land tenure as they persist;
and in terms of present needs, such as adequate land, capital, help in
development, organization of markets, and similar considerations. Such
a policy must, however, be based on full security of titles on a customary basis; and the formulation of a plastic system with possibilities
for development. Improvements in agricultural methods or system of
tenure, which are not completely divorced from the old, are not a crass
breach of continuity. Also a policy is needed for those Natives who
have lost contact with the tribal system and who are in line with modern economic conditions.

We can analyze now some of the best accounts of land tenure as
found in the work of Dr. Hunter and Dr. Mair. From Dr. Hunter's
valuable examination of tribal tenure among the Pondo, one general
principle can be stated. After she has given an excellent analysis of the
old system of ownership, which in fact still survives in the old institutions and controls the practice of magistrate and headman alike,[43] she
tells us in conclusion that in "Pondoland there has been comparatively
little change in the working of the system of land tenure since contact
with Europeans, because there is not yet a serious shortage of land."[44]
This seems simple and obvious, and yet the obvious is very often disregarded in scientific argument and statesmanship alike. In many parts
of Africa untenable conditions have arisen simply because we have
deprived the Natives of the bare essentials of any sound human existence.

Again, the conditions as regards land and resources in Pondoland
teach us first of all that new legal systems will work well as long as
there is a sufficient margin for gradual reorganization. They teach us
also that the routine as well as the sentimental attachment to the old
system have an extraordinary tenacity, and that they can also adapt
easily to new forms of technique, and that they do not stand in the
way of rural advancement. The study of land tenure in Pondoland also
raises the question of whether it is necessary to reconstruct a zero
point. In fact the old system, the new modifications, and gradual elements of change exist side by side and can be studied in actual field
work carried out on the realities. What is characteristic in this area is

43. Hunter, *op. cit.*, pp. 112–117.
44. *Idem*, p. 116.

African Land Problems

African Land Problems 131

that European infringements and interests have not been allowed to encroach too much upon the legitimate claims of the Natives. Compare what Dr. Hunter has to say about land conditions in other parts of Africa, where there is dissatisfaction over lack of land.[45] It will be easily seen that the real problem in culture change does not lie in details of mechanism and technicalities of law but in the consideration of how a minimum of natural wealth must be left to the Native, and how he must be assisted in his natural development by modern methods with due regard given to European interests.

Equally instructive in her researches on land tenure is Dr. Mair in her book, *An African People in the Twentieth Century*. The projection of her data onto the threefold charts (pp. 132–133) advocated in this book will enable us to bring out the most important points in her argument.

The original European intentions were embodied in the Uganda Agreement of 1900. It expressed on the one hand genuine administrative good-will of enduring value and on the other a desire of the British administration "to provide a perpetual safeguard for existing native rights" (A1). Now in all this there was no clash of interests, and we had a common factor in European intentions which were fully in harmony with African interests. It might thus have been a confirmation of the *status quo*. Since the old system safeguarded Native rights fully, the obvious thing would have been to study it, standardize it with as few modifications as were necessary and advisable; to translate it into terms compatible with our legal verbiage and principles; and to give it that elasticity which all constitutional enactments introducing change should have. This would have satisfied A1 and C1.

But the reform in land tenure was not in effect a wise and careful preservation of existing rights. Instead of codifying these, an arbitrary system based on European ideas and doctrines was imposed (A2). The personal rights of holdings were given to 3,700 freehold owners (A2), thus creating individual titles unknown in the previous Native system and vesting these in a small number of large landholders (B2). This legal arrangement introduced not only a small class of landowners with large estates but also a number of workers without legal rights. It also dissociated ownership of land from any governmental functions and responsibilities which had previously existed between those who actually worked the soil and those who supervised them.[46] It thus created ownership without responsibility (B2); it created titles to land without the obligation of its effective use. In so far as we indulge

45. *Idem*, pp. 556, 560.
46. *Vide* Mair, *op. cit.*, p. 198.

HISTORICAL BAGANDA LAND TENURE

A	B	C
WHITE INFLUENCES, INTERESTS, AND INTENTIONS	PROCESSES OF CULTURE CONTACT AND CHANGE	SURVIVING FORMS OF TRADITION
1. The 1900 Act, aiming primarily at safeguarding existing indigenous rights. The tenure by individual freehold granted to Kabaka and chiefs as best instrument.*	1. The common factor: in European intentions to safeguard; and Native attachment to soil and appreciation—sentimental, economic, and political—of its value. (The retention of C1 and its validation by legal recognition would have satisfied A1 and C1.)	1. The old system (then in full vigor, and persisting even now), combining economic use by cultivators with political dependence and mutual services, did *de facto* safeguard all the indigenous rights and interests.
2. Creation of large-scale estates in freehold possession of landlords, on European model—disregarding: clan lands; interests of peasants.	2. The avoidable, radical change of land tenure opened up a set of possible maladjustments, due to discontinuity with old system and disregard of old rights. (Little data recorded on this.) Trouble over clan rights arose (of minor importance according to Mair). Peasants seem to have been little exposed to hardships in the past, since they suffer little now (see following Chart).	2. Certain lands were not actually owned by the chiefs but held by them, under conditions, in trust for the peasants. Clan heads had special privileges. Peasants had services to perform but were looked after by their chiefs.
3. The economic development of the colony by indigenous enterprise [which provided safest foundations for A1] also changed value and nature of land into commercial asset through: cash crops and money economy. Direct connection with world markets.	3. Apparently there was resistance to it and friction over the constructive policy of cotton growing (details not recorded).	3. No cash crops, no money. No connection with markets (except in slave trade).

* According to Buell's data, we see at first vague recognition of private property for Kabaka and his chiefs. Then gradually (1900–1907) the rights of the 3,700 owners were defined as freehold in the sense of European law. The real point is that a policy was followed which was against sale. But did the chiefs ever want to alienate to non-Natives, and were they stopped by the administration?

PRESENT-DAY CONDITIONS IN BAGANDA LAND TENURE

A	B	C
WHITE INFLUENCES, INTERESTS, AND INTENTIONS	PROCESSES OF CULTURE CONTACT AND CHANGE	OLD SYSTEM AS IT NOW WORKS
1. "Perpetual safeguard of Native rights" still maintained by administration (little alienation; no encouragement of White settlement). But there is not sufficient information on events and policies since 1900.	1. (All questions resulting from attempts at alienation to Europeans or Asiatics, or straw-man ownership—but little data given.) Integrally little change, since A1 largely maintained, and A2 largely a dead letter.	1. Alienation—such as shifting from old to new territories and overcrowding—would produce greatest dislocation. But is *de facto* survival of old framework and most of its internal workings.
2. Working of European imposed legal system by British administrative machinery. Individual tenure to chief. Attitude of administration toward these maladjustments (information insufficiently explicit on surface of effective contact).	2. Legal scope for large-scale holdings. Ownership without responsibility; titles without obligation to use. Tenacity of traditional system, still dominating change, safeguards against maladjustments (see B3).	2. Surviving up to the present day are indigenous land tenure welding tillers to land; economic use; political duty; reciprocal services between owner-chief and tenant.
3. No prevision of possible maladjustments; no provision made to remedy them. Collateral factors in creating maladjustment are development of cash crops, introduction of money; raising of standard of living.	3. Maladjustments: speculation in land; sales and leases for profit; absentee landlordism; eviction and exploitation of tenants. (All these occur, but on diminutive scale.)	3. Ideal of good chief and landlord; survival of old modes of life (living on land; coöperation). These forces of old regime prevent at present maladjustments on large scale in B3.
4. Disregard of clan system and collective claims to land.	4. Artificial litigation due to incomplete anthropology in outlook of European settlement. Legal use of mythologies.	4. Hereditary clan lands; claims by heads of *Butaka*. The twofold mythical version. Religious and sociological functions of clan heads.
5. Coöperative banks; development of thrift and coöperation.	5. Gradual change in titles by acquisition of small holdings.	5. Old ties of kinship unity. Influences of local heads (which could be used to foster these tendencies).

in any retrospective criticism of White intentions here, we must stress the fact that the framers of policy *did* consider that all land belongs to the Native population. They did realize that even though it was not in actual use at the time it might become useful and would be exploited. They thus envisaged an economic policy of development, and this fact is most important.

Dr. Mair gives us a full account of the old system of land tenure which still works today, and this is done without reconstructing any imaginary zero point. For one of the most illuminating results of her field work consists in the fact that many of the old institutions of the Baganda have shown an enormous tenacity. She thus was able not only to define the old system but to tell us explicitly that it is at work even now. "At present 'old school' and up-to-date methods can be observed side by side. Their new rights did not at first affect the quasi-paternal attitude of the old chiefs." [47] Thus the old methods, the legal machinery of the European imposed system, the action of European administration and courts, and the phenomena of change can be studied concurrently. And this is just the method of inquiry and of marshaling the evidence which we have advocated here. We may say that certain activities still persist from the old tradition, as well as the indigenous land tenure which welds the tiller to the land and economic use to political obligations and residence (C_2).

Here again, Dr. Mair is able to signal a few abuses, dangerous tendencies, and maladjustments looming in the future. The sources of these are due to "the conception of land as a private possession at the complete disposal of the individual owner" (A_2).[48] This, hand in hand with the adoption of a money economy, made land a source of profit through leasing or sale (B_2 and B_3); "while the assignment of land to individuals and their heirs in perpetuity" [49] made land a source of speculation without any responsibilities attached. Occasional cases of absentee landowners who are acquiring tastes beyond what the offerings of their faithful followers can satisfy; [50] cases of extortionate and ruthless exploitation of tenants; and a new financial agent who calls himself a "trader in miles" and deals chiefly in "shortage certificates" [51] —such are the symptoms which may possibly develop into serious

---

47. *Idem*, p. 168.

It is not clear, however, whether this "at first" is based on historical evidence obtained from living informants or whether it is reconstructed. Dr. Mair sometimes mixes up the 1900 stage with present-day conditions.

48. *Idem*, p. 166.

49. *Ibid.*

50. *Idem*, p. 169.

51. *Idem*, p. 171.

maladjustments. Fortunately, these symptoms are as yet small and sporadic. The reasons for this are not far to seek.

The chief of them is that "land is so plentiful that speculation is not worth while." [52] Dr. Mair also states that at present "it is they [the younger landlords] who are in a position to exploit, and their efforts are kept in check both by government action and by ample areas of available land." [53] In fact, the mistake committed by most people from Lord Lugard downward in contrasting African communism with European individualism, that is, in not recognizing that the so-called individualism is an unfortunate and pathological by-product of a double allegiance—legal, ethical and economic—has led to the neglect of the point of view brought out by Dr. Mair:

One cannot help wishing that European teaching did not lay quite so much emphasis on the advantages to the individual of commercializing his possessions, and that there was more place in it for the growth of a spirit of corporate loyalty, not, indeed, to the church or king—that is sufficiently stressed—but to the smaller group with whom he is in constant contact in the life of the village.[54]

Another important protection is that the "disposal of land to non-natives is strictly controlled." [55] As long as land is plentiful, the danger is not imminent. The very reason for the limited occurrence of maladjustment in land tenure is obviously the fact that the old system, its safeguards, and moral obligations still fully dominate the situation. Landlordism is mitigated by usages more in conformity with the old order. Apparently all Natives are perfectly aware of how land tenure worked in the past, of the advantages and disadvantages of the old compared with the new system; of new landlords as compared with the government as landlord. "One hears the advantages of living on government land, where the annual rent is the only obligation, weighed against the fact that there a man who fails to pay his rent is evicted at once." [56] As a matter of fact, the old type of coöperation based on mutual exchange of services, the old ambition to live on the land among the peasants and rule them well, is still the strongest moral,

52. *Idem*, p. 167.
53. *Idem*, p. 276.
54. *Ibid*.
55. *Idem*, p. 167.
56. *Ibid*.
Formal or nominal legal rights are mostly in abeyance. "Even such *butaka* (hereditary clan lands) as have remained in the hands of their original owners, are registered in the name of one man only, and he has the full legal rights to dispose of the land without consulting the rest of the group. I know of no case where this has been done, but the possibility has caused apprehension . . ."

political, and economic force among the people. "The position of the Great Chief living among his people still represents the highest flight of human ambition." [57]

What are the practical and specific criteria of guidance to be derived from this evidence? First and foremost we can say that the new legal system which imposed a European pattern of land tenure can still be readapted by giving more and more validity to some of the old restraints, by reviving duties of land ownership as an inherent part of privileges. This tendency would run parallel to the reform in the administrative system recommended by Dr. Mair in her other book, and to the making of the Uganda system into a real form of Indirect Rule, that is, running the whole constitution on lines of customary Native law. [58] Again, and this on Dr. Mair's own advice, "the best possible safeguard against the future exploitation of the peasants consists in the acquisition of small holdings." [59] This is not a fanciful suggestion but a statement of a trend which has produced 16,000 registered landowners as compared with the 3,700 original registered allottees. [60] Through educational influence, through the foundation of coöperative societies, and direct financial loans, this trend could be strongly encouraged.

In all this we see that the treatment *de facto* used by Dr. Mair of studying European intentions, African systems, and phenomena of change side by side is identical with the one here explicitly advocated. It leads to the discovery of what we have termed the common measure of the working of these forces. Here it is the economic reality of land as a commodity to be used and not to be exploited in speculative ventures. The honesty of the European side has been proved by the exclusion of alien purchases; on the Native side there is the desire of any and every African to keep the land. European administration has also furthered the development by the introduction of economic crops. Thus the common measure is to be found in the use of land as a source of wealth on the one hand, and as a powerful force through the establishment of mutual obligations, rights, and dependencies between the landowners and tenants on the other. The benefits of the soil ought to be derived by those who live on it and coöperate in

---

57. *Idem*, p. 168.
58. Mair, *Native Policies in Africa*, pp. 169, 173–175.
59. Mair, *An African People in the Twentieth Century*, p. 170.
60. Dr. Mair could, however, have used greater care in synchronizing contemporary events. A shaking off completely of the historical obsession might have led her not to confuse 1900 with 1931, and to have given a clearer analysis of the surface of effective contact, which could have been obtained through field work rather than by a perusal of documents, and so kept apart the facts of Columns C and B and A and B.

working and managing it, and not by those merely in possession of legal claims. What survives from the old system is the good citizenship resulting from the combination of mutual dependence of headman and his subjects and their common work on the land. The new administrative regime with its legal definition of land as a mere individual asset divorced from all responsibilities and duties, together with the introduction of cotton growing as a money-making device, and with all the possibilities of speculation under the new monetary system—all these have created conditions adverse to the concurrent working of land exploitation and the exercise of citizenship. It is not in the interest of any administration to introduce speculation and to destroy citizenship. Without any ethical or metaphysical conceptions, we can maintain that good citizenship is a great cultural asset, and that in the linking up of coöperation with mutual duties there is something of the old system which ought to be safeguarded, since it still is a very strong moral force and should if possible be given a legal basis.

The above discussion of land tenure and the enumeration of the rights of Natives emphasize that not only must the bare necessities of existence be respected by law but a certain surplus conforming to the local level and its tendencies to develop must be granted. This level the anthropologist can define in terms of individual and family constitution; in terms of objects of wealth, ceremonial display, and expenditure on public works. In so far as we destroy security of tenure, we also destroy life. We have only to think of the plight of the Australian Aborigines and of the North American Indians to realize what such a policy has entailed in the past. In so far as the group enters as an essential factor into coöperation and enterprise, it must neither be destroyed nor degraded. Obviously in Africa the old tribal level cannot remain what it was, though for the time being it may survive in some places. This level must sink or rise, and the system of land tenure and territorial adjustment ought to be framed so as to be adjustable to a higher level.

XII

INDIRECT RULE AND ITS SCIENTIFIC PLANNING

THERE are few subjects in applied anthropology which are as interesting to the ethnologist as that of Indirect Rule, for in this policy we have a practical recognition that Native institutions work. The anthropologist, as one who has analyzed and realized the importance of indigenous African cultures, is therefore likely to be in sympathy with supporters of Indirect Rule for those regions where tribal authority has not yet been undermined.[1]

The motives which move a European administration to introduce Indirect Rule are partly those of expediency and efficiency and partly enlightened liberalism. It is cheap, it is practical, and it promises to produce a minimum of friction and dissatisfaction, for it involves rule with the consent of the majority of those governed, and the maintenance of as much as possible of the Native authority instead of its destruction.[2]

It does not require a great deal of anthropological insight to recognize that authority can best be wielded by those who for ages have been and are regarded as the legitimate rulers; who are surrounded by an imponderable aura of prestige; who have religious functions, and who are believed to possess magical powers. A mechanism which has been used for centuries and which is adapted to the environment, to the social milieu, and to tribal institutions is probably better than a

1. In *An African Survey* "Indirect Rule" is used "to denote the system by which the tutelary power recognizes existing African societies and assists them to adapt themselves to the functions of local government" (p. 413). For the broader implications of Indirect Rule, the reader is referred to Dr. Mair's *Native Policies in Africa*, where she points out that "the real meaning of Indirect Rule cannot be summed up in the phrase, 'Find the Chief.' It consists in an understanding of the structure of native society and the interrelation of its parts, which precludes the possibility of assuming that it can be suddenly modernized from outside, and at the same time reveals the points at which changed circumstances call for readjustment, and the bases on which necessary innovations can be firmly established" (p. 15). Dr. Mair sums it up even more succinctly as "the progressive adaptation of native institutions to modern conditions" (p. 56). For further discussions of Indirect Rule, see Margery Perham, *Native Administration in Nigeria* (1937), and "A Restatement of Indirect Rule," *Africa* (July, 1934); also Buell, *The Native Problem in Africa*. Ed.

2. Indirect Rule has sometimes been criticized as a refusal to undertake responsibilities, and as a drag on progress. An answer to these charges has been made by Miss Perham in the article cited above, and also by Dr. Mair who, in her book, has not only analyzed the conditions necessary for the application of Indirect Rule but has also pointed out very cogently that they do not exist in many cases, for example, in such areas as Swaziland, Bechuanaland, and Basutoland (*vide op. cit.*, pp. 55–63).

rapidly improvised alien type of rule. There is also no doubt that the chief and his councillors who are traditional, who know the people and who are known by them, who are conversant with customary law, and who can look at things from the Native point of view will be able to administer better than a casual nominee of the government. Between, however, the recognition of these principles and the correct and clear knowledge of how to draft the tribal constitution, there is a long way to go. It is in the provision of such an anthropological diagnosis of how the present constitution works or fails to work that the anthropologist can be of use.

What are the points which have to be settled before Indirect Rule is introduced into an area where chieftainship has been disregarded completely for a long time, that is, treated as dead? The first question, obviously, is whether it is really alive to the extent at least that its recognition will make it a working institution.[3] If it is alive, then it is important to ascertain its character, how it functions, what are its charter, its religious foundations, its legal, military, and economic bases. Here the pertinent question is whether the "old system" as it operates now is applicable to modern conditions. For it must be remembered that even though Native chieftainship was able to fulfill its functions under the old traditions, it cannot now, unchanged, carry out the tasks which the coöperation with Europeans and the maintenance of law and order impose on it in a situation of culture contact. Again, it may be that what survives of the old chieftainship is even less capable of effective work. Therefore in drafting a constitution it is essential to know whether each aspect of the institution is suited for further development and growth; whether it is compatible with probable trends.[4] In short, there must be an assessment of forward policy. Equally, it would be necessary to inquire into what might contain germs of maladjustment—whether an ambitious chieftain would at once misuse his powers, or an unscrupulous one withstand the temptations of corruption.

Indirect Rule represents a new development and cannot be regarded as an agglomerate of elements. Its charter is the re-shaping of sovereignty, of the sources of executive power, and of finance and reve-

3. Dr. Hunter points out that among the Pondo, although the powers of the chief have been curtailed, he still has much of his prestige, and that the government has been requested to restore his authority (*op. cit.*, pp. 429–430). Similarly in Northern Nigeria, Tanganyika, and Northern Rhodesia there was no difficulty in finding the legitimate chiefs when Indirect Rule was introduced.

4. Lord Hailey raises the question whether a form of Indirect Rule would be in the interests of Union Natives, if it is envisaged that eventually they will be admitted to full citizen rights. He also points out that the system would be unsuitable for the large Native populations in urban areas in the Union (*op. cit.*, p. 530). Ed.

CHIEFTAINSHIP
POLITICAL CONSTITUTION UNDER INDIRECT RULE

A	B	C
WHITE INFLUENCES, INTERESTS, AND INTENTIONS	PROCESSES OF CULTURE CONTACT AND CHANGE	SURVIVING FORMS OF TRADITION
1. Indirect Rule: Government by coöperation and partial delegation of power; recognition, suppression, and creation. Clear understanding of issues; specific knowledge in each case of what still exists.	1. Concrete charter of Indirect Rule. Definition of European sovereignty (international, military, judicial, fiscal). Definition of old powers restated and new functions imposed. Definition of mechanisms of coöperation by which control and responsibility are shared.	1. Tribal Native constitution. Chief; chief-in-council; hierarchy and Native local government. Aspects: a) mythological charter b) religious foundations c) revenue d) law giving and judging e) military power f) sovereignty (all these not in pristine form but already affected by contact).
2. Military and Police: Pax Britannica; military sovereignty abolished; British Army with African man power. Police under European control.	2. Gradual readjustment of old military; reorganization to new purposes; a territorial army? framework for economic enterprise? (regiments and age-grades in E. and S. E. Africa). N.B., sociological and psychological problem: how to compensate for cultural value of militarism. Problem of substitution.	2. Rudiments of military organization remain. Native awareness of loss of sovereignty. Financial, political, and sentimental deficiencies due to this. (Slave and slave traffic, trade in ivory, other forms of war booty.)
3. Public finance: Native treasuries reorganized. Taxation old and new. Principle of gradually improved budgeting (development of indirect economic exploitation of natural resources; European enterprise as a political factor).	3. Problems of balance in loss of old revenues and development of new ones; in budgeting for new types of expenses (relatively simple in N. Nigeria; very intricate in S. Nigeria and E. Africa, especially re "forced labor"). New indigenous sources of revenue.	3. Native Treasuries: the revenues still operative and the revenues abolished (war, slavery). Expenditure necessary in the carrying out of administrative, ceremonial, and legal duties. Prestation in kind and labor.
4. Administration of justice: Recognition of Native law, with provisos.	4. Problem of development of Native capacity in legislation. Difficulties arising	4. Legislative function of African chief, usually constitutionally restrict-

A	B	C
WHITE INFLUENCES, INTERESTS, AND INTENTIONS	PROCESSES OF CULTURE CONTACT AND CHANGE	SURVIVING FORMS OF TRADITION
Need of new powers of legislation which can be delegated to Native chiefs. Division in jurisdiction, leaving final control to Europeans but most of the handling to the Natives. European lawyers, administrative officers.	from Native courts having to administer justice under twofold control of Native and European principles. New types of property; marriage and family; professions, wages, labor.	ed. Existing principles of Native civil and criminal law.
5. Politics and Religion: Influence of missions undermining power of chief. Indirect Rule must support chief.	5. Conflict between missionary and administrator substantially due to conflict between new loyalty and political efficiency. Conversion of chief solves some of difficulties—at a price.	5. The organic unity between political and religious power: chief as rain maker and master of fertility. Chieftainship and ancestor worship.
6. Education: European schooling indispensable to Indirect Rule. Schooling through missions may undermine old system. Possible adaptation of indigenous institutions.	6. Education on two fronts. Implanting of European points of view re economic, judicial, and fiscal outlook. Necessity of maintaining old tribal law. Problems: differential education of chief and commoner. Difficulties created by educated African, upstart, demagogue.	6. Native systems of training: domestic; age grades; apprenticeship in arts and crafts, and citizenship.

nue. As a complex experiment, it has nothing at all in it which has been directly taken over from the older cultures. It represents the gradual growth of collaboration; it is the reality which is flanked, as it were, by two cultural responses; it depends on both, but develops by its own laws of growth and has its own determinism.

Here as in our discussion of other aspects of culture change, we should construct a three-column scheme on the following brief. In Column A, we should state first the general principle or ideal under which the colony is administered. Thus all colonies labeled "Indirect

Rule" can be defined as those where an attempt is being made at using indigenous monarchies, chieftainships, Native assemblies and courts; giving them the support and sanction of European administration; defining their functions, rescinding some of them, amplifying others, and introducing new ones. The question would then arise as to how complete a knowledge (anthropological) the framers of each local constitution have of the political constitution of the tribe; and what difficulties and complications the enormous diversity of systems introduces in a given colony, such as Tanganyika. It would also be important to know the degree of latitude given to the provincial or district commissioners in applying the principles in each particular case. Such documents as the instructions given by the secretariat to its officers about the concrete way of applying principles must be known to the fieldworker.

In column B the investigator would have to study by field work the actual working of the administration by White and Native alike; their coöperation and conflicts. Here the study of the working of the *lukiko* (King's Council) among the Baganda, of the chief's councils on the Kilimanjaro, of the illiterate chiefs of Northern Rhodesia or Tanganyika, or of the highly educated chiefs of Barotseland and Swaziland would be necessary.

Column C would be reserved for the working of unacknowledged political institutions and influences. The anthropologist would also observe here the extent, as well as the function, of such Native customary law (e.g., witchcraft) as still goes on *sub rosa* in opposition to the White Man's constitution.

So as not to argue in a void, let us turn to the concrete case of Northern Rhodesia where Indirect Rule was introduced in 1929, after a regime of direct administration. Here we have a problem of exceptional importance, and by good fortune there was a competent anthropologist on the spot. Dr. Richards worked among the Babemba soon after the inauguration of the new policy. At the time of its introduction, there were many critics within and outside the administration. Chieftainship had remained unrecognized for about a quarter of a century, and it was not really possible to assess how far it could bear the burdens imposed upon it. As a matter of fact, the experiment proved a success, certainly in Northeastern Rhodesia. "This is an area in which the institution of chieftainship far from being moribund, is very much alive, even after years of direct administration." [5] Under such conditions, there was obviously a very good foundation on which Europeans

5. Richards, "Tribal Government in Transition," *Journal of the Royal African Society*, suppl. to XXXIV (1935), 21.

and Africans could coöperate. Europeans wanted to use African political machinery—with certain reservations; the Africans, who in spite of adverse circumstances still remained faithful to the old political regime, showed not only their intention but also their determination to use it. The common factor therefore existed: i.e., the joint determination to have power and authority vested in the chief, under European control; for European control had been as fully accepted by the African as it had been taken for granted by the European.

And yet, though the experiment on the whole has been an unquestionable success,[6] it has proved so in spite of, rather than because of, the handling of the situation by Europeans. Theoretically, once the policy had been decided upon, all that there was to do was to study the old system, prune it, establish control, and supplement lacunae. Did the European administration do this? Not quite.

Let us analyze theoretically the problems that existed at the time of the introduction of Indirect Rule; and let us present diagrammatically (pp. 140–141) the issues, the ideal procedure, and the type of advice which the anthropologist could have given at the time.[7]

Under A1 we have listed the intention of the colonial power to introduce Indirect Rule, in recognition of the fact that Native authority under European control is desirable; that it constitutes the ideal of government with the consent of the governed; and is the most effective and cheapest to run. In other words, the Europeans intend to govern, using the existing machinery of C1. This machinery of the old days is still very much "alive," although minus its military aspect, and despite the restriction of economic resources, the abolition of slavery, the exodus of male labor, and the growth of competing and hostile elements, such as missionary influence and the rise of Native progressives. Thus under B1, our prognosis as to the common factors of administrative coöperation, we have the concrete charter of Indirect Rule, the definition of European sovereignty; the old powers of Native authority restated and new functions imposed; the definition of the mechanisms of coöperation by which control and responsibility are shared. In short, the European administration professes to utilize what the Africans are *de facto* using, i.e., the established authority of the tribe. This implies that the prognosis is favorable in the measure

6. Richards, *op. cit.*, p. 22.

7. Unfortunately, Malinowski left (with the exception of a few pages of typescript) only penciled notes on problems of administration. These I have rearranged and made into a consecutive text. He did, however, leave several charts, and I have incorporated the material from these into the main text. While I have had to add phrases and sentences for the sake of style and continuity, the ideas, criticisms, and conclusions are all his. Ed.

in which the European drafted constitution conforms to C1. Here, as Dr. Richards has shown in her field work among the Babemba, the position of the chief, the *Citimukulu*, has still its mythological and religious sanction; he still exercises certain functions, maintains his court, and has the assistance of certain functionaries, such as the *bakabilo* (hereditary councillors) and the *bafilolo* (elders of the chief's court), though all this is in a greatly diminished form.[8]

Yet—and the point must be emphasized—the European administration in devising its policy is not a free agent. For besides the ideal of Indirect Rule, and the existence of real and active conditions which make this ideal fully realizable, there are a number of factors which limit its application. In Column A we must include certain conditions which prevent a revival of Native authority in its pristine form. First and foremost, there is the abolition of war and slavery, of forced labor and the tribute of ivory; the imposition of the Pax Britannica, and the rescinding of the chief's powers of life, death, and mutilation over his subjects (A2). While the rudiments of military organization still exist, and the Natives are aware of a surrender of sovereignty in this regard (C2), nevertheless, as a phenomenon of Column B, the suppression of the chief's right in these matters is inevitable (B2). We could, however, advise some gradual readaptation of the old military organization to new purposes, perhaps as a framework for economic enterprises, public works, and education, as in other parts of Africa. Primarily, we are faced with the problem of substitution, of a compensation for the cultural value of militarism.

When we turn to fiscal policy (A3), we must register the necessity of financing the recognized Native administration. This will entail some reorganization of Native treasuries, the retention of some old forms of taxation, and the introduction of new ones; the principle of gradually improving budgeting; and the development of Native economic exploitation of natural resources. For the implementation of this program, direct reference must be made to C3, to the revenues still available, to those which have been abolished with the passing of war and slavery. A careful assessment must be made of the expenditure necessary for the carrying out of the administrative, ceremonial, and legal duties of the chief and his court. Hence in B3 we are faced with the problem of devising means of balancing the loss of old revenues and of developing new ones; the budgeting for new types of expenditure on the basis of new indigenous sources of revenue.

Under the administration of justice (A4), the charter of Indirect Rule involves the recognition of Native law with certain provisos; the

8. Richards, *op. cit.*, pp. 5–20.

need for new powers of legislation which can be delegated to Native chiefs; and finally, a division in jurisdiction, leaving the ultimate control in the hands of Europeans but most of the handling to Natives— in short some reorganization of courts. Here, too, field work would have to be carried out which would bring to light existing principles of African civil and criminal law (C_4), and the extent of the judicial powers of the chief and councillors, with the recognition that the legislative functions of the African chief are usually constitutionally restricted, and that there never was legislative activity comparable to the new duties envisaged for him.[9] The implementation of Indirect Rule in this respect would thus create the problem of developing Native capacity for legislation (B_4), and it would also have to face the difficulty arising from Native courts having to administer justice under a twofold control of Native and European principles, since new types of property, new forms of marriage, new professions, the introduction of a money economy, and labor for Europeans have all created conditions not covered by the old law. Here we may state, as a general principle governing the phenomena of Column B, that since all moderating influences tend to undermine the power of Native authority, compensations along other lines will be necessary.

At various times in the course of this book reference has been made to the effect on tribal economy of the exodus of its male labor to the mines. This obviously has its repercussions on the chief's authority, prestige, and resources. Here we must emphasize again that the administration cannot act entirely as a free agent, that is, without regard for other European vested interests. Whatever the desirability or justice of the latter, they must be taken into account by the anthropologist as determining factors in the total culture contact situation. It must therefore be recognized in the economic field that while Europeans are in the country, a certain amount of alienation of land will be necessary for their requirements; that mines will need labor and also the inculcation of an appreciation of money on the part of the Natives, if the latter are to be induced to work. With the control that might be exerted over conditions in the mines, with the checks that might be imposed on the departure of large numbers of men from the reserves, with the utilization of some of their wages for the development of Native agriculture, and with the necessity for sufficient lands, we have already dealt. Therefore, while the presence of European vested in-

9. However, as an indication of adaptability it should be noted that Dr. Richards in her field work heard the *bakabilo* deliberately reinterpreting tribal tradition to meet an issue raised by modern conditions, and was amazed by their shrewdness in this respect (*vide op. cit.*, p. 14).

terests in the country will obviously affect the practical implementation of the policy of Indirect Rule, there must be safeguards for Native interests and a compromise reached where these clash with European attempts at exploitation.

This conflict between European parties is especially relevant when we consider the contradiction inherent in a situation in which the policy of Indirect Rule must support the power and prestige of the chief, while at the same time the influence of the missions undermines it. If we turn to C5, we find that in Native culture there was and in fact still is an organic unity between political and religious power, that the chief acted as rain maker and master of fertility, and that there was a strong nexus between chieftainship and ancestor worship. For instance, Dr. Richards says on this point: "Moreover he (the paramount chief) had in his own person, by virtue of his descent from a line of tribal ancestors, supernatural powers over the welfare of the whole land. The depth of this Bemba belief . . . is, I believe, even now the ultimate sanction for the supreme authority of the *Citimukulu* over his whole territory." [10] Hence in B5 we are faced with the conflict between the old and the new loyalties; with the problem of how to utilize the old spiritual forces without producing stagnation. The conversion of the chief to Christianity solves some of the difficulties at a price, but where this does not occur, or where the bulk of the people still adhere to the traditional beliefs, the problem persists. The demand for a more enlightened policy on the part of missionaries in regard to ancestor worship, the necessity of recognizing its ethical values, has already been stressed elsewhere in this book.

Finally, some European schooling is indispensable to Indirect Rule, while at the same time there should be, wherever possible, an adaptation of indigenous institutions in this regard (A6).[11] The anthropologist must also register the possibility of conflict and of the undermining of the old system wherever missions have control of the schooling. Under the old system (C6), there existed Native methods of training, both within the kinship groups and through age grades, apprenticeship in arts and crafts, and the gradual acquiring of citizenship. Hence for a discovery of the common factor between European intentions and forces and the Native system it is obvious that there must be education on two fronts: that is, the implanting of the European point of view for those situations where Natives are brought into contact and co-

10. *Idem*, p. 7.

11. For a fuller discussion of Malinowski's views on education see "Native Education and Culture Contact," *International Review of Missions*, Vol. XXV (1936); and also "The Pan-African Problem of Culture Contact," *American Journal of Sociology*, Vol. XLVIII, No. 6 (1943). Ed.

operation with Europeans in economic, judicial, and administrative matters; on the other hand, there is the necessity of maintaining the old tribal law. Here one of the main questions is the differential training for chiefs and commoners, the obviating of those situations in which an illiterate chief has to deal with an educated clerk, with educated commoners, and upstart demagogues.

From this discussion of the principal factors which have been placed in synoptic form in our diagram, some of the main dangers are clear. If the Europeans plan in the void without reference to African realities, there is no real basis for coöperation. On the other hand, if policy is limited entirely by what exists now in African culture, then rigidity and no possibilities for development must be the result. Thus the basis for the drafting of a program is the fullest understanding by Natives of European aims; and by Europeans of Native difficulties, in so far as the object is to create in Native authority a devoted and dependable ally, controlled, but strong, wealthy, and satisfied.

When, however, we examine the policy as it was eventually formulated and carried out, we find many conflicts and inherent contradictions. Native courts were set up for jurisdiction over all cases except murder and witchcraft; Native authorities were appointed with limited powers to issue orders; but no Native treasuries were created, and the chief therefore had no rights over any portion of the tax, though the government did envisage granting a measure of control later.[12]

Now while in the interests of administrative expediency the government may have to reserve to itself jurisdiction over murder and witchcraft, there is still much ground for legitimate criticism. Little or no trouble was taken to ascertain what Native authority meant. Dr. Richards is correct in saying that "in most parts of Africa finding the chief has been considered equivalent to establishing indirect administration. We have not taken the trouble to study the working of the whole political machine of which the institution of chieftainship itself formed part."[13] In Northern Nigeria and Tanganyika, however, the approach was a much broader one. But the question remains a mystery why no systematic inquiry was carried out in Northern Rhodesia. What should have occurred: the appointment of the chief-in-council with the necessary financial foundations, a definition of the powers and assistance given to the chief by European and Native councillors, was therefore never realized. The existence of the bakabilo, the hereditary councillors who have important religious and political functions, was ignored; and in so far as the chief in practice tends to do without

12. Richards, *op. cit.,* p. 5.
13. *Ibid.*

their aid, one of the most important elements in tribal government necessary for the functioning of Indirect Rule is weakened.[14]

However it speaks much for the tenacity of the old system that in spite of its nonrecognition by the government it continues to play some part in the new administrative set-up. The chief has maintained his court, though in a greatly emasculated form; the bafilolo, court officials who help the chief in his duties, still contribute to the creation of his prestige; and the *bamushika*, formerly captains in the chief's army, now act as trusted messengers, and hence make possible some coördination of activities throughout the various districts.[15] Yet all such court functionaries are reduced in number, for the chief lacks the means to pay, feed, and reward them.

The European government has not recognized the fact that the chief's religious duties constitute a most important sanction for his authority; and though on the face of it there is no reason why he should not fulfill these *sub rosa*, he would nevertheless risk the opposition of powerful missions in the area.[16] Here then we have the conflict between missionary and the chief as a religious head, a clash of right with right. One might suggest that the government at least prohibit bullying acts of violence, such as the destruction of Native shrines and the molestation of national relics, thus affirming the principle of liberty of conscience and the abolition of all inquisitions.

In the economic sphere, we have already discussed the position of the chief at the time of the introduction of Indirect Rule, and the measures which should have been taken to provide a solid financial foundation for his administration. He has to have adequate resources to meet the expenses of supporting classes of officials and a court, the rewarding of followers, and the dispensing of hospitality, for his prestige did and does now depend on his role as a generous ruler with a large capital and a plentiful supply of food.[17] We recognized in our theoretical analysis that some of his revenues are lost to him irretrievably, namely, those from slavery and war, while gone too are his monopoly over ivory, his powers to exact tribute, and to call for *mulasa* (labor) for his gardens. Finally, he has to compete with a new moneyed and educated class among his subjects.

What measures have been taken by the government to assist the chief financially and to compensate for the losses of his former economic resources? We find that the chief's salary (in 1937) was £60 a

14. *Idem*, p. 20.
15. *Idem*, pp. 8-10.
16. *Idem*, p. 17.
17. *Ibid.*

year! With this sum a ruler of 150,000 subjects has to meet fixed annual liabilities for the clothing of his wives and domestic servants, the
clothing and education of his children, the wages of an administrative
staff, and religious dues. The balance he has left is about £19, a smaller
sum for him to spend than has the average cook in his district.[18]
Obviously there is an urgent need here for a translation of some of
his old vested interests into new assets, some share in taxation, or some
means of making a voluntary levy.

Finally, little has been done to cope with the situation in which an
illiterate chief and his illiterate councillors have to rule over subjects
some of whom are semi-educated. Dr. Richards has narrowed down
the alternatives to a choice between the old hereditary council imbued
with a sense of public service, or the appointment of a younger body
of men, better educated, but with little tradition of public responsibility.[19] But one may ask whether the issue is one between education
and traditional prestige. Why not have both? [20] Some forward policy
is required, which will enable the chief and his advisers to assume the
responsibility entailed in governing a people whose customs are changing; to decide on reforms; to initiate regulations and to exercise some
control over financial questions. In the light of Dr. Richards' material
the introduction and implementation of Indirect Rule in Northern
Rhodesia can be seen as a dynamic process of adaptation, of compromise, and replacement; as an interchange and mutual reaction. We
have not been concerned with constructing any zero point of change,
nor have we been able to regard the situation as "an integral whole,"
though here, if anywhere at all, that conception might be applied.

The facts in our chart demonstrate that a common factor exists between the *prima facie* White intentions and Native realities. But the
belief that the policy merely involves finding the chief and installing
him has been revealed as a fallacy. Dr. Richards in her brilliant article
has demonstrated the value, vitality, and political utility of Native
authority but has also indicated that it has been impaired, not only

18. *Idem,* pp. 20, 26.
Dr. Richards has also worked out a specimen budget of the Paramount Chief for the
year 1934, which reveals the pitiful inadequacy of his salary (*vide,* pp. 25–26).
Dr. Richards has also suggested that the financial difficulties of the chief might be
solved either by increasing his salary or by payment of his councillors. Certainly "the
economic position of the chief is the key to most problems of Indirect Rule" (p. 24).
19. *Idem,* pp. 22–23.
20. Schools for chiefs exist in Gambia, Sierra Leone, and Nyasaland. Those in Tanganyika have recently been abandoned, as it was considered no longer necessary to
reserve special instruction for the families of chiefs. There was also some doubt
whether it was in keeping with the spirit of Native institutions to mark the chiefs out
as a separate class. *Vide* Hailey, *An African Survey,* p. 1257. Ed.

by the exigencies of vested interests such as the White demand for labor and the opposition of missions, but also by the failure on the part of the administration to acquire a full knowledge of Native institutions. While we can appreciate the fact that the administrator is not an anthropologist, it is obvious from her account that many mistakes have been unnecessary, as for instance the failure to make adequate provision for the economic needs of the chief during a transition period. Dr. Richards, as a functional anthropologist, has been able to go further, and on the basis of her analysis point out the need for official recognition of the bakabilo; she has revealed the sources of the chief's prestige, his sense of responsibility, and the checks which the old system imposed on his power.

The real problem of contact, which the anthropologist is bound to assess, depends then largely on how to strengthen financially, politically, and legally the present-day chief under present-day conditions. His role as the main officiating priest in tribal ancestor worship, in the harvest ceremonies, and in rain-making magic, raises the difficult and complicated problems about the relation of the missions to the old religion. Here the questions to be asked are: how far do the missionaries directly fight the influence of the chief, while the administration tries to bolster it up? In what concrete activities does this twofold influence find expression?

While the table with its synoptic presentation of argument is but an instrument, it has shown clearly the system of coördinates which every efficient fieldworker has to use; it has thrown into relief the three phases of culture change in administration; it has shown the relation of the European brief, the principles of policy, to legislative implementation and practice, and to the observed effects on Native life, welfare, maladjustment, and possibilities for development.

XIII

THE PROMISE OF CULTURE CHANGE AND
ITS FULFILLMENT

IT MAY be well to summarize briefly some of our results, to disentangle one or two of the main principles, and lay down what appear to me to be the main lines on which the anthropology of culture change ought to be developed. Let us do this point by point.

1. Applied and Theoretical Anthropology

Here, perhaps, the most important thing is the clear realization that all really sound theory is bound in the long run to be practical. On the other hand, the fieldworker who remains in touch with the vital issues of a practical nature will receive through this a stimulus to his work and inspiration, which will inevitably lead him to fruitful theoretical discoveries. We have found that strictly scientific method demands that the anthropologist should study what is: the facts as they now exist and the processes which are going on at present. Since all these processes belong to the domain of culture change; since they all involve efforts of White administration, missions, and industrial entrepreneurs, obviously the subject matter of the new anthropology becomes increasingly identified with that of practical interests. Purely indigenous cultures no longer exist in Africa or anywhere else. The observable facts include White influences as well as Native traditions.

The developments in modern anthropological theory also lead us toward a more rigid distinction between important facts and processes on the one hand and curiosities and antiquarianisms on the other. Anthropology has now turned to the study of such subjects as economics, political institutions, land tenure and labor; and it has set out to discuss problems of marriage, the family, kinship, and sex on a functional basis: that is, the study of how these institutions work, what they contribute to the demographic strength of a tribe and to its social and legal stability. Here again the scientific approach comes much nearer to the practical. The intelligent administrator, missionary, or educationalist has come to recognize that a full and disinterested knowledge of the facts is part of his duty, as well as an efficient help in his work; while in the study of religion, magic, and even witchcraft the modern anthropologist has recognized that he is not dealing with a specifically archaic type, with something that interests him merely as an illustration of primitive, useless modes of thought. On the contrary, we have come to perceive that universally human, moral, dogmatic, and social attitudes are to be found in African ancestor worship or in their belief in one Godhead, in their religious appeal to natural forces, and in their fears, hopes, and misgivings connected with magical practices. Here also the anthropologist working on functional lines can assist the missionary in showing him what is the common measure of primitive and developed religions. The main lesson from the new theological approach is that in evangelization it is possible to fulfill and not merely to destroy.

One of the main implications of the recent developments in the science of man is the tendency to look forward as well as back to the past; to consider the *terminus ad quem* of culture change, the forward trend of the new social, intellectual, and moral reintegrations of things African under the influence of European culture. In this also, there is no divergence of interest between the practical man and the student. Modern anthropology is taking the functional or instrumental point of view. It deals with the workings of organized human activities or institutions as means to the satisfaction of needs. From this point of view the *rapprochement* between practical interest and theoretical study is real and inevitable. On the theoretical side, culture change allows us to examine such institutions as Native land tenure, Native systems of marriage, or Native belief in witchcraft under conditions of strain. The aspects of any institution which show a great resistance to change are revealed *prima facie* to be the strongest and the most fundamental.

"Conservatism" consists partly in the wide ramifications of certain beliefs such as ancestor worship, in the great adaptability of certain superstitions such as witchcraft and magic. For instance, the fact that *lobola* or bride-price has endured persecution, adverse legislation, and a good deal of denunciation from the pulpit, and that it has had to be reinstated by European legislation and acknowledged by missions, is to a modern anthropologist an opportunity for study and a disclosure of the first magnitude. The adaptability of witchcraft and its special developments under culture contact are another example of how changing conditions enable us to gain an insight into the working of ideas and practices submitted to adverse pressure. To the practical man on the other hand this knowledge is equally important. Had the missions understood that the bride-price had nothing to do with any economic transaction, that its function was not to enslave the woman nor to give her over as a chattel to her husband, they certainly would not have committed the capital mistake of prohibiting it, and thus would not have exercised an unfortunate influence on Native marriage and family.

The functional discussion of change, of those forces which tenaciously resist all attempt at modification under conditions of contact— all this has recently become the main task of scientific anthropology, and it has always been the concern of the practical man in Africa. Nowadays when science has to invade so many domains of practical import; when it is becoming increasingly apparent that we shall have to replace the rough and ready methods of "muddling through" by a clear and systematic study of the issues, it seems inevitable that the practical man should meet the anthropologist half way, especially since the latter has already come so much nearer to practical problems and to the practical handling of change. To hope that once the above truths are fully recognized the coöperation will become ideal would certainly be far too sanguine. Administration, missions and industrial enterprises have been established for a long period. It would be expecting a superhuman attitude if they welcomed gladly a newcomer with a relatively short history to his credit. They are and have been vested interests for ages in the past, and while there is an increasing tendency for them to admit the value of anthropological studies for certain problems, nevertheless many of the questions discussed in the previous chapters do constitute a challenge to the existing fundamental lines of policy in missionary attitudes, labor, and territorial appropriation. A cogent scientific proof that the South African Bantu has not enough land given to him is extremely easy to formulate. It is in fact unnecessary, for the truth has been recognized in acts of Parliament, in resolution, and in statements of specially appointed commissions. But the only effective solution goes against the vested interests of a minority now in power. The voice of the anthropologist here is even more inconvenient than the harangues of the pro-Native, because he speaks in terms of fact and figures, and of the irrefutable logic of measuring ends and protestations against the means adopted for their achievement. But this cannot silence the voice of the scientific research worker, especially when he knows that what he has to say is the truth, and a truth of immense practical importance for the future, however distant.

2. The Historical and Functional Approach

From a purely theoretical point of view, a most important *leitmotiv* of the preceding argument was the distinction between "history dead and buried" and "tradition alive and at work." This distinction I have tried to make clear in several concrete analyses. Those who have disengaged the theoretical point of view from the actual discussion of the facts will not be likely to misunderstand the position here advocated. In the first place, it is not in any way an attempt to attack the value of historical research and historical reconstruction. But it must be clearly recognized that when we study the Zulu, the Babemba, or the Masai of today we are no longer observing the pre-European conditions of the tribe but a phenomenon of culture change. An account of the tribal constitution, the laws, beliefs, and customs of the Natives as they existed in their pristine fullness, is the result of a specific elaboration. The methods used for that are different from those of mere observation. Above all it must be kept in mind that what the "old men of the tribe" tell us about the past can never be scientific or historical truth, since it is always affected by sentiment, by retrospective regrets, and longings. Such statements have to be treated as mythology, albeit mythology of the recent past.

And here comes another *caveat*. So-called "historical" explanations are very often based on the *post hoc, ergo propter hoc* fallacy. The legitimate historical explanation is only possible when we can trace the development of an institution and establish continuity in function as well as in form. African slavery and slave raiding are still molding certain attitudes toward rank within the tribe and the ideas of tribal superiority as between one section and another of a mixed group. To appreciate this influence we can either study the present-day ideas only, or else we can compare past conditions with present ones. In many ways the second proceeding would be of very great value in supplementing the first in theory and perhaps also in practice. But this would only be the case if we could obtain a full functional picture of pre-European conditions with regard to slavery, land tenure, marriage, law, or ancestor worship. In most instances this is now quite impossible, for as I have had occasion to repeat again and again, the past records are so defective from the scientific point of view that they are completely worthless for the purposes of comparison with the present as studied in scientific field work.

3. *Principles and Methods of Contact Study*

The main system of approach which we have developed here involves first of all the subdivision of the problem into several constituent aspects, and then the correlation of these at every point of correspondence. In order to give body and precision to this approach, we have elaborated the device of synoptic schemes. The columns contained therein refer to the factors in the situation, which can to a large extent be considered as self-contained and independent provinces of study. Column A, the various European influences, interests, and intentions, is one of our main entries. In our Column B we have listed a set of facts belonging to what, in another place, I have called the "anthropological no-man's-land," since it was ignored by the older anthropologists as not being purely tribal, and would have escaped the sociologist or historian as being not quite European. Here belong all the spheres of activity in which Africans and Europeans coöperate: where the European has to draw the African into his concerns and often work side by side with him; and where the African has to take cognizance of his White leader or guide. The labor on mines or plantations, the school in the bush, or the African college, the Native court of law administered under White supervision, a Native suburb in Johannesburg or Nairobi—such phenomena as well as their legal, economic, religious, or educational interrelations belong to Column B *par excellence*. In Column C we have indigenous institutions which continue to function either *sub rosa* or ignored by Europeans. To these three columns others might be added: a flanking column for A of European influences from overseas; a Column D for the reconstructed past; and finally, a Column E which points toward the future and which would include forces of reaction and new Native institutions.

4. *Criteria of Value and of Practical Guidance*

Here once more the purely scientific or theoretical approach allows us on the one hand to state definitely that it is the duty of sound research to provide such criteria, while on the other hand we can also stress the fact that in this the research worker need not either resort to the historical comparison of pre-European conditions or yet introduce any moral or specifically normative values. Here once more the instrumental approach, the concept of cultural developments as being means to ends, is of profound significance. The principle that institutions such as marriage or the family, agriculture or land tenure, have special functions to fulfill is quite sufficient for the provision of definite criteria. The fieldworker has, of course, to be completely a-political. In his work and in his theories he must not be either an agnostic unable to see eye to eye with the missionaries, or an ardent sectarian who despises all other versions of Christianity but his own and is unable to see any value in African religion. He must not be either a communist or a fascist, a dogmatic believer in the unique race-value of the Nordic or an ardent pro-Native. He must be able to assess the aims, ideals, and practical task of any European undertaking. Take, for example, missionary work: the implanting of the new sexual morality and the raising of standards of ethical conduct need not be by any means uncongenial to the scientific fieldworker. In fact, his knowledge of the drives, inclinations, and difficulties connected with the reproductive instinct, as well as his appreciation of its value in building up stable marriage and effective family organization and also in leading to important cultural developments, allows him to meet the missionary on common ground. But he would have to insist that "sexual morality," when it is taken as a cultural reality applicable to a wide range of conditions, cannot be defined in terms of a special Christian sect.

In problems of Native labor, the anthropologist would again have to stress the European need for an effective labor supply, one which has to be considered as a fact and as a relevant fact in the situation. But he must insist as well that in the long run a type of *Raubwirtschaft* in Native labor—the spoliation of reserves and the undermining of the tribal economy, hence food supply, hence nutrition—must defeat the ends of even the idea of Africa as a White Man's Country founded on Native labor. In land tenure, a good deal of perfectly sound and painless surgery could be carried out in some areas in the way of cutting out wider reserves from European lands for the Natives, if public opinion could be made to see the facts; facts, that is, which reveal that the Bantu is a necessary partner to the European; that through Bantu prosperity the European will thrive; and that Bantu poverty and misery are as infectious as any contagious disease.

In short, a fuller knowledge of the facts and a better presentation of them would result in criteria of value or rules of guidance which would be objective and of direct practical utility, without going beyond the legitimate scope of field work and its interpretation. It is hardly necessary to add that the comparison of the present with the reconstructed past is entirely useless for scientific, that is, practical, criteria of guidance. What we need are more data with regard to the European side of the equation, the reservoir of indigenous traditions, the mechanisms of change and contact, and finally, the phenomena of indigenous but new African movements. This is the more essential since neither the "Native" nor the "African" nor the "Bantu" exists. The study must be made in every region, in every type of contact-community—the urbanized, those connected with farms, those where Natives are used as mine labor, or on plantations or tribal reserves. In each of these cases field work has to be carried out with reference to the new principles, problems, and methods inherent in the study of culture contact.

5. *The Lines of Tribal Renegation and Integral Rebuff* [1]

In summarizing our discussion in this book, there remains one important aspect to be taken up. In our analysis of the new phase of transition, the sphere of culture change, the concept of two lines which divide it from the European and African world respectively has been prominent. One of them appears, looking from the historical perspective, at the initial stages of detribalization. The African crosses the line of the First Tribal Renegation when he adopts some of the new ways imposed by European culture. The acceptance of Christianity; the entry into a European school; the labor contract or enlistment in military, police, or administrative employments mark this transition.

The forces which determine this step result from the fact of impact. All the early European influences, from the display of the overwhelming superiority of armed force or economic power to educational advice or moral uplift, constitute the drives of the first transition. This inevitably implies the renunciation of one or another African activity or value. The Native in a way enters into a new covenant. For value received and hopes inspired, he has to abandon some of his old allegiances and ways; he has to forswear some of his old faiths and convictions. He takes up new ways of life and even a new disguise in dress, manner, and personal habits. He enters this avenue, fascinated by the qualities, power, wealth, and general prestige of things European. The ultimate goal implied, if not explicit, is to become, if not European, then at least a master or part-master of some of the devices, possessions, and influences which in his eyes constitute European superiority. How far and in what way is he ever allowed to approach this goal? He may go as far as a European or American university; receive such academic degrees as become a member of a highly skilled profession. But when he returns to his own country, he will have to go through a dramatic experience. He will discover that the status of equality, or even equivalence, in matters legal, economic, political, and social, is denied him.

In the life-story of every assimilated African, and in the development of any African detribalized community or group, there comes a moment in which the second line or barrier makes its inevitable and

1. This section, apart from one or two insertions from other manuscripts, has been taken with but minor changes from the last part of Malinowski's "Modern Anthropology and European Rule in Africa," Reale Accademia d'Italia, Fondazione Alessandro Volta, Estratto dagli Atti dell' VIII Convegno (Rome, 1938; published, 1940), XVIII, 19–23, 25–26. Ed.

inexorable appearance. We may call it the Line of Integral Rebuff from total assimilation. Concretely, it exists as color-bar legislation, the principle of racial discrimination, the fundamental rule of the Grondwet; or the policy of permanent segregation. It separates as by a deep rift the community of partly assimilated Africans from that of their White neighbors.[2]

The African response at this second line is as important and as inevitable as the European initiative. Since Africans cannot share the ideals, interests, and full benefits of coöperative activities with the Whites, they naturally fall back on their own systems of belief, value, and sentiment. To be a mere carbon copy is not satisfactory as a substitute for all the African had initially to give up. The more independent, far-seeing, and sensitive he is, the stronger will be the reaction. Its strength depends on the degree of ambitions, hopes, and expectations raised at the first crossing. It is also commensurate with the degree to which the African has advanced along the line of assimilation. The trenchant literature of educated Africans on Bantu grievances, on the hardships imposed upon the Native intelligentsia, clearly documents this reaction. But it is not confined to the intelligentsia alone. All over Africa we observe the growth of nationalism: tribal, regional, or Pan-African. It finds expression in the separatist Christian churches; in the demands for the return to tribal authority; in the reintroduction of *lobola* marriage, of initiation ceremonies, and of Native family and kinship systems. Such elements of the old culture as female circumcision; the ritual attitude toward cattle; African music, dancing, and entertainments, are being revived with a secondary, almost ethnographic interest in racial history, customary law, and the artistic and intellectual achievements of their race. The African thus is forced at least spiritually to recross the first line and to reaffirm many of the tribal values abandoned at the first crossing.

This sophisticated nationalism or tribalism can still draw full strength from the enormous residues of old tradition. For African institutions, memories, and sagas are alive not only in the tribal areas but also among the partly detribalized communities.

The existence of these two schematic lines—that of promise and attraction by European ideals and that of rebuff—and their relation to each other constitute perhaps the strongest determining force in the phase of contact and transition in those areas where there are a

2. It is not implied that this line of rebuff from total assimilation always takes the form of legislative discrimination. It would be true to say, however, that even where the paramountcy of Native interests is recognized in law and largely in practice, many European settlers do have racial prejudices and refuse to meet the Africans on terms of equality. Ed.

considerable number of permanently settled Europeans. Both lines are established by Europeans. Both are, let us realize, inevitable. And yet there are a number of questions which arise immediately we become aware of this reality. Is it not possible to establish a fuller and more adequate common measure between promises and their fulfillment; between fulfillment and the real needs of the Africans? The African may not obtain what he hoped for. Yet he may receive enough to compensate him for the things relinquished and lost. For the African, as we have seen, has to give up some of his political rights, social status, his secure standard of living, as well as his old supernatural protections on which he had relied against fate and misfortune. What does he receive in return? Very often but a shadow of what he has been promised and what he needs, and not even a fair equivalent of what he has lost.

Compare a Native family in a tribal reserve with its counterpart in an urban location or squatting on a European farm. The tribal household is organized on the old standard of life, which satisfies customary needs and requirements and is adapted to indigenous economy. The inmates know the amount of work which they will have to put in, the resources on which they can rely, and the rewards which hard work and skill will give them. There is little room for unfulfilled promise and for the shocks of unexpected disproportion between effort and satisfaction. Even natural catastrophes are usually foreseen in the tribal code of behavior.

The detribalized household has been accustomed to a much higher standard of living, essentially inherent in the fact that it is a partly Europeanized family, with the needs of education, clothing, hygiene, and cleanliness. The new household is entirely dependent economically on wages—and here comes the fact demonstrated from field work in most of the districts where large detribalized groups have been studied. Family budgets show that the expenditure necessary for the maintenance of the new standard very often, almost invariably, exceeds the regular earnings of the father of the family. This means that malnutrition, insufficient training for the children, and overwork in additional pursuits, often illegal, by wife and children create conditions incompatible with the raised standards of expectations, with health, and with all the advantages implied in the charter of transition. Here we have facts which can be verified objectively and which show how the discrepancy between promise and fulfillment leads to conditions which are sociologically unsound.

Take another example: in many districts Native agriculture is being improved by teaching, demonstrations, a supply of implements, and veterinary care for cattle. In the same area, however, the Natives have been deprived of such large portions of their tribal lands that any development is made illusory, while improved methods of cattle breeding result in destructive overstocking. We know already that the educated African receives a type of equipment preparing him for professional or technical work which is made impossible for him either by color-bar legislation or simply by the fact that he cannot exercise his profession through lack of customers, since the detribalized Natives live on artificially low wages.

In all this, I am simply pointing out some of the forces which, wisely controlled, may ensure a normal and stable development but when mismanaged may lead to dangerous consequences. We do not need to underrate the value and necessity of African assimilation and progress, and the influence of education and Christianity. But it is clear that wise colonial statesmanship in matters administrative, educational, economic, and religious will do well to assess the potentialities and dangers implied in the relation between things promised and things given. For the disproportion between the hopes raised and the advantages promised to the African when he is induced to cross the line of tribalism and the realization which he receives at the barrier of racial discrimination is the main problem to be considered.

I suggest that first and foremost it would be well to unify, coördinate, and harmonize various policies. For we have already noted the considerable discrepancy between the enthusiasm of good-will and educational zeal, and the existence of the color bar; between the requirements of the settler and the activities of the agricultural department, which may develop economic ambitions beyond the legitimate scope of their realization. Whenever Europeans plan the settlement of large portions of any colony, segregation and color bar become inevitable. This ought to be remembered by the enthusiastic minority of good-will, who may involuntarily raise high hopes through such doctrines as the Brotherhood of Man, the Gospel of Labor, and the possibilities of assimilation through education, dress, manners, and morals. If, from the outset, it were possible to make quite clear in preaching the gospel of civilization that no full identity can ever be reached; that what are being given to the Africans are new conditions of existence, better adapted to their needs but always in harmony with European requirements, the smaller would be the chances of a strong reaction and the formation of new, potentially dangerous nationalisms.

But this admonition to the minority of good-will is not all that the anthropologist has to say. He has also a few words to address to that majority of European interests who naturally are not directly concerned with the welfare of the Natives. Big enterprise, organized trade, and most of the administrative agents act primarily under European imperatives. Through their influence the measure of fulfillment is often made inadequate to the promise of the enthusiastic minority.

The anthropologist must therefore also insist that a substantially increased measure of real and tangible benefits is necessary, in the interests not only of the African but also of the White community. In the long run, African and European interests converge because stable and effective rule by a minority can only be founded on the real satisfaction, prosperity, and welfare of the Native subjects.

Substantial grants of administrative autonomy, of land reserved for Natives, of financial assistance, and of cultural independence are as sound an investment for the success of European rule as they are beneficial to the Native. Any colonial power, but especially one actually faced with the task of reorganizing or planning its policies, might well study the history of South and parts of East Africa, and draw the scientific conclusions that the facts force upon us.

It is hardly necessary to affirm here explicitly that no criticism of the specifically British methods of colonial policy is implied in the statements of this book. As one acquainted in Africa with British territories only, I had naturally to deal with culture contact in that area. Colonization is never a simple and smooth process. The nation with the longest and most extensive experience in these matters has necessarily had to solve some of the most difficult problems by the method of trial and error—for its own benefit and that of others. As a Pole born and bred, I may be allowed to say here that in my opinion the British colonial system is second to none in its capacity to learn from experience, its adaptability and tolerance, and above all, in its genuine interest in the welfare of the Natives.

The ethnographer who has studied culture contact and has assessed its active forces, its potentialities and dangers, has the right and duty to formulate his conclusions in a manner in which they can be seriously considered by those who frame policies and those who carry them out. He also has the duty to speak as the Natives' advocate. But he can go no further. Decisions and the practical handling of affairs are outside his competence. His primary duty is to present facts; to develop concepts theoretically valid and practically useful; to destroy fictions and empty phrases, and thus to reveal the forces and factors which are relevant and active. Through comparative study he can discover and define the common factor of European intentions and of African response. He can lay bare the sources of maladjustment. These, at times, he will find are due to real intrinsic conflict of interests; at times they arise from faulty assessment of African realities; or again, from almost adventitious misunderstandings. His advice may be sometimes a clear warning, or sometimes a contribution to a piece of constructive planning. Knowledge gives foresight, and foresight is indispensable to the statesman and to the local administrator, to the educationalist, welfare worker, and missionary alike. The discovery of long-run tendencies; the capacity of foreseeing and forecasting the future in the light of full knowledge of all the factors involved; competent advice on specific questions—these are the tasks of the contact-ethnographer as a practical expert.

BIBLIOGRAPHY

AFRICA [1]

Africa, Vol. VIII, No. 4, 1935, contains articles on witchcraft and culture change by E. E. Evans Pritchard, G. St. J. Orde-Browne, F. Melland, and A. I. Richards.

BEEMER, H., "The Development of the Military Organization in Swaziland," *Africa*, Vol. X, Nos. 1 and 2, 1937.

——— "Notes on the Diet of the Swazi in the Protectorate," *Bantu Studies*, Vol. XIII, 1939.

BROWN, G., and HUTT, A., *Anthropology in Action*, 1935.

BUELL, R. L., *The Native Problem in Africa*, 2 vols., 1928.

FORTES, M., "Culture Contact as a Dynamic Process," *Africa*, Vol. IX, No. 1, 1936.

GLUCKMAN, M., "Analysis of a Social Situation in Modern Zululand," *Bantu Studies*, Vol. XIV, 1940.

HAILEY, M., *An African Survey*, 1938.

HUNTER, M., *Reaction to Conquest:* Effects of Contact with Europeans on the Pondo of South Africa, 1936.

——— "Methods of Study of Culture Contact," *Africa*, Vol. VII, No. 3, 1934.

MAIR, L. P., *An African People in the Twentieth Century*, 1933.

——— *Native Policies in Africa*, 1936.

——— "The Study of Culture Contact as a Practical Problem," *Africa*, Vol. VII, No. 4, 1934.

MEEK, C. K., *Law and Authority in a Nigerian Tribe*, 1937.

Methods of Study of Culture Contact in Africa, Memorandum XV, International Institute of African Languages and Cultures, 1938. This contains articles by A. T. and G. Culwick, M. Fortes, M. Hunter, L. P. Mair, A. I. Richards, I. Schapera, G. Wagner, and B. Malinowski on culture change.

PERHAM, M., *Native Administration in Nigeria*, 1937.

——— "A Restatement of Indirect Rule," *Africa*, Vol. VII, 1934.

——— ed., *Ten Africans*, 1936.

READ, M., "Tradition and Prestige among the Ngoni," *Africa*, Vol. IX, No. 4, 1936.

RICHARDS, A. I., *Land, Labour and Diet in Northern Rhodesia*, 1939.

——— "Tribal Government in Transition," *Journal of the Royal African Society*, Supplement, Vol. XXXIV, 1935.

——— "Anthropological Problems in North-Eastern Rhodesia," *Africa*, Vol. V, No. 2, 1932.

1. This bibliography is not exhaustive, and covers only those books and articles to which reference was made in Malinowski's manuscripts. Ed.

RICHARDS, A. I., "The Village Census in the Study of Culture Contact," *Africa*, Vol. VIII, No. 1, 1935.

—— and WIDDOWSON, E. M., "A Dietary Study in North-Eastern Rhodesia," *Africa*, Vol. IX, No. 2, 1936.

SCHAPERA, I., *Western Civilization and the Natives of South Africa*, 1934.

TINLEY, J. M., *The Native Labour Problem of South Africa*, 1943.[2]

THURNWALD, R., *Black and White in East Africa*, 1936.

VAN DER HORST, S. T., *Native Labour in South Africa*, 1942 [2]

WESTERMANN, D., *The African Today*, 1934.

GENERAL [3]

American Anthropologist, Vol. XLV, n. s., No. 2, 1943, contains articles on acculturation by R. Kennedy, M. Mead, J. Steward, R. Benedict, C. Kluckhohn, and R. Linton.

ELKIN, A. P., "Anthropological Research in Australia and the Western Pacific, 1927–1937," *Oceania*, Vol. VIII, No. 3, 1938.

HERSKOVITS, M. J., *Acculturation: A Study of Culture Contact*, 1938.

—— "Memorandum for the Study of Acculturation," *American Anthropologist*, Vol. XXXVIII, n. s., 1936.

—— "The Significance of the Study of Acculturation for Anthropology," *American Anthropologist*, Vol. XXXIX, n. s., 1937.

—— "Some Comments on the Study of Culture Contact," *American Anthropologist*, Vol. XLIII, n. s., 1941.

HOGBIN, H. I., *Experiments in Civilization*, 1939.

KEESING, F. M., *Modern Samoa*, 1934.

—— *The South Seas in the Modern World*, 1941.

LA FARGE, O., ed., *The Changing Indian*, 1942.

LINTON, R., ed., *Acculturation in Seven American Indian Tribes*, 1940.

LORAM, C. T., and McILWRAITH, T. F., *The North American Indian Today*, 1943.

MEAD, M., *The Changing Indian*, 1932.

REDFIELD, R., "Culture Changes in Yucatan," *American Anthropologist*, Vol. XXXVI, n. s. 1934.

REED, S. W., *The Making of Modern New Guinea*, 1943.

STANNER, W. E. H., "The Aborigines," *Some Australians Take Stock*, 1938, J. C. Kevin, ed.

SUTHERLAND, I. L. G., ed., *The Maori People Today*, 1940.

THOMPSON, L., *Fijian Frontier*, 1940.

2. Books consulted by the author.

3. This is not a comprehensive list of books and articles on culture change, but covers only those to which reference has been made by Malinowski or by myself. Ed.

ARTICLES ON CULTURE CHANGE BY B. MALINOWSKI

"Practical Anthropology," *Africa,* Vol. II, No. 1, January, 1929.

"Race and Labour," *The Listener,* Supplement No. 8, 1930.

"The Rationalization of Anthropology and Administration," *Africa,* Vol. III, No. 4, 1930.

"Native Education and Culture Contact," *International Review of Missions,* Vol. XXV, October, 1936.

"The Scientific Basis of Applied Anthropology," Reale Accademia d'Italia, Fondazione Alessandro Volta, Estratto dagli Atti dell' VIII Convegno, Rome, 1938; published, 1940.

"Modern Anthropology and European Rule in Africa," Reale Accademia d'Italia, Fondazione Alessandro Volta, Estratto dagli Atti dell' VIII Convegno, Rome, 1938; published, 1940.

"Anthropology of Changing African Cultures," *Methods of Study of Culture Contact in Africa,* Memorandum XV, International Institute of African Languages and Cultures, 1938.

"The Present State of Studies in Culture Contact," *Africa,* Vol. XI, 1938.

"The Present State of Studies in Culture Contact," *Africa,* Vol. XII, No. 1, 1939.

"The Dynamics of Contemporary Diffusion," résumé in *International Congress of Anthropological and Ethnological Sciences,* Copenhagen, 1939.

"Introduction" to *Fijian Frontiers* by Laura Thompson. Studies of the Pacific, No. 4, published by the American Council of the Institute of Pacific Relations, 1940.

"Introducción" to *Contrapunteo Cubano del Tabaco y el Azucar* by Fernando Ortiz, Havana, 1940.

"The Pan-African Problem of Culture Contact," *American Journal of Sociology,* Vol. XLVIII, No. 6, 1943.

INDEX